GRAMMAR
AND BEYOND

John D. Bunting
Luciana Diniz
with Randi Reppen

4B

CAMBRIDGE
UNIVERSITY PRESS

CAMBRIDGE UNIVERSITY PRESS
Cambridge, New York, Melbourne, Madrid, Cape Town,
Singapore, São Paulo, Delhi, Mexico City

Cambridge University Press
32 Avenue of the Americas, New York, NY 10013-2473, USA

www.cambridge.org
Information on this title: www.cambridge.org/9780521143288

© Cambridge University Press 2013

First published 2013

Printed in Hong Kong, China, by Golden Cup Printing Company Limited

A catalog record for this publication is available from the British Library.

ISBN 978-0-521-14301-1 Student's Book 4
ISBN 978-0-521-14323-3 Student's Book 4A
ISBN 978-0-521-14328-8 Student's Book 4B
ISBN 978-1-107-60409-4 Workbook 4
ISBN 978-1-107-60410-0 Workbook 4A
ISBN 978-1-107-60411-7 Workbook 4B
ISBN 978-1-107-67297-0 Teacher Support Resource Book with CD-ROM 4
ISBN 978-0-521-14343-1 Class Audio CD 4
ISBN 978-1-139-06188-9 Writing Skills Interactive 4

Art direction, book design, layout services, and photo research: Integra
Audio production: John Marshall Media

Contents

3 parts including 10 units

Introduction to *Grammar and Beyond*

Grammar and Beyond is a research-based and content-rich grammar series for beginning- to advanced-level students of North American English. The series focuses on the grammar structures most commonly used in North American English, with an emphasis on the application of these grammar structures to academic writing. The series practices all four skills in a variety of authentic and communicative contexts. It is designed for use both in the classroom and as a self-study learning tool.

Grammar and Beyond Is Research-Based

The grammar presented in this series is informed by years of research on the grammar of written and spoken North American English as it is used in college lectures, textbooks, academic essays, high school classrooms, and conversations between instructors and students. This research, and the analysis of over one billion words of authentic written and spoken language data known as the *Cambridge International Corpus*, has enabled the authors to:

- Present grammar rules that accurately represent how North American English is actually spoken and written

- Identify and teach differences between the grammar of written and spoken English

- Focus more attention on the structures that are commonly used, and less attention on those that are rarely used, in written and spoken North American English

- Help students avoid the most common mistakes that English language learners make

- Choose reading and writing topics that will naturally elicit examples of the target grammar structure

- Introduce important vocabulary from the Academic Word List

Grammar and Beyond Teaches Academic Writing Skills

Grammar and Beyond helps students make the transition from understanding grammar structures to applying them in their academic writing.

In the Student's Books

At Levels 1 through 3 of the series, every Student's Book unit ends with a section devoted to the hands-on application of grammar to writing. This section, called Grammar for Writing, explores how and where the target grammar structures function in writing and offers controlled practice, exposure to writing models, and a guided but open-ended writing task.

At Level 4, the most advanced level, the syllabus is organized around the academic essay types that college students write (e.g., narrative, cause and effect) and is aimed at teaching students the grammar, vocabulary, and writing skills that they need in order to be successful at writing those kinds of essays.

Online

Grammar and Beyond also offers *Writing Skills Interactive*, an interactive online course in academic writing skills and vocabulary that correlates with the Student's Books. Each unit of the writing skills course focuses on a specific writing skill, such as avoiding sentence fragments or developing strong topic sentences.

Special Features of *Grammar and Beyond*

Realistic Grammar Presentations

Grammar is presented in clear and simple charts. The grammar points presented in these charts have been tested against real-world data from the *Cambridge International Corpus* to ensure that they are authentic representations of actual use of North American English.

At Level 4 vocabulary charts present words and phrases that naturally occur in each writing genre.

Data from the Real World

Many of the grammar presentations and application sections in the Student's Book include a feature called Data from the Real World, in which concrete and useful points discovered through analysis of corpus data are presented. These points are practiced in the exercises that follow.

Avoid Common Mistakes

Each Student's Book unit features an Avoid Common Mistakes section that develops students' awareness of the most common mistakes made by English language learners and gives them an opportunity to practice detecting and correcting these errors in running text. This section helps students avoid these mistakes in their own work. The mistakes highlighted in this section are drawn from a body of authentic data on learner English known as the *Cambridge Learner Corpus*, a database of over 35 million words from student essays written by nonnative speakers of English and information from experienced classroom teachers.

Academic Vocabulary

Every unit in *Grammar and Beyond* includes words from the Academic Word List (AWL), a research-based list of words and word families that appear with high frequency in English-language academic texts. These words are introduced in the opening text of the unit, recycled in the charts and exercises, and used to support the theme throughout the unit. The same vocabulary items are reviewed and practiced in *Writing Skills Interactive*, the online writing skills course. By the time students finish each level, they will have been exposed several times to a carefully selected set of level-appropriate AWL words, as well as content words from a variety of academic disciplines.

Series Levels

The following table provides a general idea of the difficulty of the material at each level of *Grammar and Beyond*. These are not meant to be interpreted as precise correlations.

	Description	TOEFL IBT	CEFR Levels
Level 1	beginning	20 – 34	A1 – A2
Level 2	low intermediate to intermediate	35 – 54	A2 – B1
Level 3	high intermediate	55 – 74	B1 – B2
Level 4	advanced	75 – 95	B2 – C1

Components for Students

Student's Book

The Student's Books for Levels 1 through 3 teach all of the grammar points appropriate at each level in short, manageable cycles of presentation and practice organized around a high-interest unit theme. The Level 4 Student's Book focuses on the structure of the academic essay in addition to the grammar rules, conventions, and structures that students need to master in order to be successful college writers. Please see the Tour of a Unit on pages xii–xv for a more detailed view of the contents and structure of the Student's Book units.

Workbook

The Workbook provides additional practice of the grammar presented in each unit of the Student's Book. The exercises offer both discrete and consolidated practice of grammar points and can be used for homework or in class. Each unit also offers practice correcting the errors highlighted in the Avoid Common Mistakes section in the Student's Book to help students master these troublesome errors. Self-Assessment sections at the end of each unit allow students to test their mastery of what they have learned.

Writing Skills Interactive

This online course provides graduated instruction and practice in writing skills, while reinforcing vocabulary presented in the Student's Books. Each unit includes a vocabulary review activity, followed by a short text that builds on the theme presented in the Student's Book and provides an additional context for the vocabulary. The text is followed by an animated interactive presentation of the target writing skill of the unit, after which students have the opportunity to practice the target skill in three different activities. Each unit closes with a quiz, which allows students to assess their progress.

Teacher Resources

Teacher Support Resource Book with CD-ROM

This comprehensive book provides a range of support materials for instructors, including:

- Suggestions for applying the target grammar to all four major skill areas, helping instructors facilitate dynamic and comprehensive grammar classes

- An answer key and audio script for the Student's Book

- A CD-ROM containing:

  - Ready-made, easily scored Unit Tests

  - PowerPoint presentations to streamline lesson preparation and encourage lively heads-up interaction

Class Audio CD

The class audio CD for each level provides the Student's Book listening material for in-class use.

Teacher Support Website

www.cambridge.org/grammarandbeyond

The website for *Grammar and Beyond* contains even more resources for instructors, including:

- Unit-by-unit teaching tips, helping instructors plan their lessons

- Downloadable communicative activities to add more in-class speaking practice

- A monthly newsletter on grammar teaching, providing ongoing professional development

We hope you enjoy using this series, and we welcome your feedback! Please send any comments to the authors and editorial staff at Cambridge University Press, at grammarandbeyond@cambridge.org.

About the Authors

John D. Bunting is a Senior Lecturer in the Intensive English Program in the Department of Applied Linguistics & ESL at Georgia State University. Prior to this, John taught EFL in Venezuela. He wrote *College Vocabulary 4* (Cengage, 2006) and worked on a revision of *Vocabulary in Use High Intermediate* (Cambridge, 2010). His research interests are corpus linguistics, vocabulary, academic writing, technology in language learning, and teacher education.

Luciana Diniz is the ESOL Department Chair at Portland Community College and an instructor. She has an MA and a PhD in Applied Linguistics from Georgia State University, and she has been teaching EFL/ESL for nearly 15 years. Luciana's research interests focus on the use of corpus linguistics in vocabulary and grammar teaching/learning. She has presented a number of papers at national and international conferences.

Randi Reppen is Professor of Applied Linguistics and TESL at Northern Arizona University (NAU) in Flagstaff, Arizona. She has over 20 years' experience teaching ESL students and training ESL teachers, including 11 years as the Director of NAU's Program in Intensive English. Randi's research interests focus on the use of corpora for language teaching and materials development. In addition to numerous academic articles and books, she is the author of *Using Corpora in the Language Classroom* and a co-author of *Basic Vocabulary in Use*, 2nd edition, both published by Cambridge University Press.

Advisory Panel

The ESL advisory panel has helped to guide the development of this series and provided invaluable information about the needs of ESL students and teachers in high schools, colleges, universities, and private language schools throughout North America.

Neta Simpkins Cahill, Skagit Valley College, Mount Vernon, WA

Shelly Hedstrom, Palm Beach State College, Lake Worth, FL

Richard Morasci, Foothill College, Los Altos Hills, CA

Stacey Russo, East Hampton High School, East Hampton, NY

Alice Savage, North Harris College, Houston, TX

Authors' Acknowledgments

In addition to our gratitude toward the many people who have collaborated in the preparation of this book, Luciana would like to thank her husband and best friend – Sergio – for his love and support. John wishes to acknowledge the insights and guidance provided by his friend and colleague, Sharon Cavusgil. He is also indebted to his wonderful wife Mayira and to Chris and James – their love and support sustain him.

Acknowledgments

The publisher and authors would like to thank these reviewers and consultants for their insights and participation:

Marty Attiyeh, The College of DuPage, Glen Ellyn, IL

Shannon Bailey, Austin Community College, Austin, TX

Jamila Barton, North Seattle Community College, Seattle, WA

Kim Bayer, Hunter College IELI, New York, NY

Linda Berendsen, Oakton Community College, Skokie, IL

Anita Biber, Tarrant County College Northwest, Fort Worth, TX

Jane Breaux, Community College of Aurora, Aurora, CO

Anna Budzinski, San Antonio College, San Antonio, TX

Britta Burton, Mission College, Santa Clara, CA

Jean Carroll, Fresno City College, Fresno, CA

Chris Cashman, Oak Park High School and Elmwood Park High School, Chicago, IL

Annette M. Charron, Bakersfield College, Bakersfield, CA

Patrick Colabucci, ALI at San Diego State University, San Diego, CA

Lin Cui, Harper College, Palatine, IL

Jennifer Duclos, Boston University CELOP, Boston, MA

Joy Durighello, San Francisco City College, San Francisco, CA

Kathleen Flynn, Glendale Community College, Glendale, CA

Raquel Fundora, Miami Dade College, Miami, FL

Patricia Gillie, New Trier Township High School District, Winnetka, IL

Laurie Gluck, LaGuardia Community College, Long Island City, NY

Kathleen Golata, Galileo Academy of Science & Technology, San Francisco, CA

Ellen Goldman, Mission College, Santa Clara, CA

Ekaterina Goussakova, Seminole Community College, Sanford, FL

Marianne Grayston, Prince George's Community College, Largo, MD

Mary Greiss Shipley, Georgia Gwinnett College, Lawrenceville, GA

Sudeepa Gulati, Long Beach City College, Long Beach, CA

Nicole Hammond Carrasquel, University of Central Florida, Orlando, FL

Vicki Hendricks, Broward College, Fort Lauderdale, FL

Kelly Hernandez, Miami Dade College, Miami, FL

Ann Johnston, Tidewater Community College, Virginia Beach, VA

Julia Karet, Chaffey College, Claremont, CA

Jeanne Lachowski, English Language Institute, University of Utah, Salt Lake City, UT

Noga Laor, Rennert, New York, NY

Min Lu, Central Florida Community College, Ocala, FL

Michael Luchuk, Kaplan International Centers, New York, NY

Craig Machado, Norwalk Community College, Norwalk, CT

Denise Maduli-Williams, City College of San Francisco, San Francisco, CA

Diane Mahin, University of Miami, Coral Gables, FL

Melanie Majeski, Naugatuck Valley Community College, Waterbury, CT

Jeanne Malcolm, University of North Carolina at Charlotte, Charlotte, NC

Lourdes Marx, Palm Beach State College, Boca Raton, FL

Susan G. McFalls, Maryville College, Maryville, TN

Nancy McKay, Cuyahoga Community College, Cleveland, OH

Dominika McPartland, Long Island Business Institute, Flushing, NY

Amy Metcalf, UNR/Intensive English Language Center, University of Nevada, Reno, NV

Robert Miller, EF International Language School San Francisco – Mills, San Francisco, CA

Marcie Pachino, Jordan High School, Durham, NC

Myshie Pagel, El Paso Community College, El Paso, TX

Bernadette Pedagno, University of San Francisco, San Francisco, CA

Tam Q Pham, Dallas Theological Seminary, Fort Smith, AR

Mary Beth Pickett, Global-LT, Rochester, MI

Maria Reamore, Baltimore City Public Schools, Baltimore, MD

Alison M. Rice, Hunter College IELI, New York, NY

Sydney Rice, Imperial Valley College, Imperial, CA

Kathleen Romstedt, Ohio State University, Columbus, OH

Alexandra Rowe, University of South Carolina, Columbia, SC

Irma Sanders, Baldwin Park Adult and Community Education, Baldwin Park, CA

Caren Shoup, Lone Star College – CyFair, Cypress, TX

Karen Sid, Mission College, Foothill College, De Anza College, Santa Clara, CA

Michelle Thomas, Miami Dade College, Miami, FL

Sharon Van Houte, Lorain County Community College, Elyria, OH

Margi Wald, UC Berkeley, Berkeley, CA

Walli Weitz, Riverside County Office of Ed., Indio, CA

Bart Weyand, University of Southern Maine, Portland, ME

Donna Weyrich, Columbus State Community College, Columbus, OH

Marilyn Whitehorse, Santa Barbara City College, Ojai, CA

Jessica Wilson, Rutgers University – Newark, Newark, NJ

Sue Wilson, San Jose City College, San Jose, CA

Margaret Wilster, Mid-Florida Tech, Orlando, FL

Anne York-Herjeczki, Santa Monica College, Santa Monica, CA

Hoda Zaki, Camden County College, Camden, NJ

We would also like to thank these teachers and programs for allowing us to visit:

Richard Appelbaum, Broward College, Fort Lauderdale, FL

Carmela Arnoldt, Glendale Community College, Glendale, AZ

JaNae Barrow, Desert Vista High School, Phoenix, AZ

Ted Christensen, Mesa Community College, Mesa, AZ

Richard Ciriello, Lower East Side Preparatory High School, New York, NY

Virginia Edwards, Chandler-Gilbert Community College, Chandler, AZ

Nusia Frankel, Miami Dade College, Miami, FL

Raquel Fundora, Miami Dade College, Miami, FL

Vicki Hendricks, Broward College, Fort Lauderdale, FL

Kelly Hernandez, Miami Dade College, Miami, FL

Stephen Johnson, Miami Dade College, Miami, FL

Barbara Jordan, Mesa Community College, Mesa, AZ

Nancy Kersten, GateWay Community College, Phoenix, AZ

Lewis Levine, Hostos Community College, Bronx, NY

John Liffiton, Scottsdale Community College, Scottsdale, AZ

Cheryl Lira-Layne, Gilbert Public School District, Gilbert, AZ

Mary Livingston, Arizona State University, Tempe, AZ

Elizabeth Macdonald, Thunderbird School of Global Management, Glendale, AZ

Terri Martinez, Mesa Community College, Mesa, AZ

Lourdes Marx, Palm Beach State College, Boca Raton, FL

Paul Kei Matsuda, Arizona State University, Tempe, AZ

David Miller, Glendale Community College, Glendale, AZ

Martha Polin, Lower East Side Preparatory High School, New York, NY

Patricia Pullenza, Mesa Community College, Mesa, AZ

Victoria Rasinskaya, Lower East Side Preparatory High School, New York, NY

Vanda Salls, Tempe Union High School District, Tempe, AZ

Kim Sanabria, Hostos Community College, Bronx, NY

Cynthia Schuemann, Miami Dade College, Miami, FL

Michelle Thomas, Miami Dade College, Miami, FL

Dongmei Zeng, Borough of Manhattan Community College, New York, NY

Tour of a Unit

Each unit presents grammar and vocabulary structures that **naturally occur** in a specific writing genre.

UNIT 5

Comparison and Contrast 1: Identifying Relative Clauses; Comparatives with *As . . . As*; Common Patterns That Show Contrast

Family Size and Personality

1 Grammar in the Real World

You will read an essay that discusses how a child's birth order in the family – being the oldest child, middle child, youngest child, or an only child – may affect his or her personality as an adult. The essay is an example of a type of comparison and contrast writing in which the ideas are organized using the block method.

A *Before You Read* How many siblings (brothers and sisters) do you have? Do you think that some of their personality traits come from the order of their birth? Read the essay. How strong are the effects of birth order, according to the information in the essay?

Birth Order and Adult Sibling Relationships

What do Jimmy Carter, Bill Clinton, and George W. Bush all have in common? In addition to being elected president of the United States, these men all share the same birth order. Each one is the oldest child in his family. In fact, many very successful people in government and business have been "firstborn" children. While there is always some
5 variation, some experts agree that birth order can have an influence on a person's personality in childhood and in adulthood.

Firstborn children often share several traits. First, in contrast to their siblings, they are more likely to be responsible, ambitious, and authoritarian. This is probably because they are born into an environment of high expectations, and they usually receive a great deal of
10 attention. They are used to being leaders, taking responsibility for others, and sometimes taking on an almost parental role.

Middle children, on the other hand, exhibit different characteristics from firstborns. They are often not as determined as firstborns. They tend to be more passive and solitary. Having to share family attention with older and younger siblings, middle children have a
15 tendency to be more realistic, creative, and insightful.

Youngest children are often more protected than their older siblings. As a result, they are more likely to be dependent and controlling. They are often as creative as middle children, but usually more easygoing and social.

64

A child with no siblings, or an "only child," also exhibits some unique characteristics.
20 While some parents worry that an only child will have difficulties socializing and making friends, studies show that an only child is just as intelligent, accomplished, and sociable as a child with siblings. In fact, some research indicates that being an only child has some benefits. These children tend to have better vocabulary, perform better at school, and maintain closer relationships with their parents than children with siblings (Petersen,
25 2010, p. 2).

Even though it is assumed that birth order dictates some personality traits, individuals can free themselves from the roles they played when they were young, but it can be difficult. According to Vikki Stark, family therapist and author of *My Sister, My Self*, change requires letting go of familiar ways of being and patiently asserting new behaviors that
30 express one's true self (Kochan, 2006, para. 10).

B *Comprehension Check* Answer the questions.

1. How are former presidents Bill Clinton and George W. Bush connected to the main idea of the text?
2. According to the writer, why are firstborn children usually more ambitious than their siblings?
3. Which of the different birth order types – firstborn, middle born, youngest, and only child – do you think has the fewest advantages in life? Explain.

C *Notice*

1 **Comparison and Contrast Writing** Complete the outline below with information from the essay. The essay is organized using the block method. In this method, the main points that describe one part of the issue are presented together in "one block" or paragraph, and the main points that describe the second side of the issue are presented in the next paragraph, and so on.

Block Method: Birth Order and Adult Sibling Relationships

Introductory paragraph. Thesis statement: Some experts agree that birth order can have an influence on a person's personality in childhood and adulthood.

Body Paragraph 1. Topic: _Firstborn children_
(1)
Personality traits: responsible, ambitious, authoritarian

Body Paragraph 2. Topic: _____
(2)
Personality traits: passive, solitary, _____, creative, _____
(3)   (4)

Body Paragraph 3. Topic: _____
(5)
Personality traits: dependent, _____, creative, easygoing, _____
(6)   (7)

Body Paragraph 4. Topic: _____
(8)
Personality traits: intelligent, _____, sociable
(9)

Grammar in the Real World presents the grammar and vocabulary structures in an **essay on a contemporary topic.**

Notice activities first draw students' attention to the **structure of the genre.**

Additional *Notice* activities help **students analyze** the grammar, vocabulary, and writing skill.

Grammar and Vocabulary charts provide clear guidance on the form, meaning, and use of the target language **for ease of instruction and reference**.

2 Grammar Follow the instructions below to help you notice and understand comparison and contrast sentences from the essay that use *as . . . as*.

1. Read the *as . . . as* sentence in the third paragraph. Are middle children likely to be equally determined, more determined, or less determined than firstborn children? Explain.
2. Read the *as . . . as* sentence in the fourth paragraph. Are youngest children likely to be equally creative, more creative, or less creative than middle children? Explain.
3. Read the *as . . . as* sentence in the fifth paragraph. Are only children likely to be equally intelligent, more intelligent, or less intelligent than children with siblings? Explain.

3 The Writing Process Underline the sentence that gives the main idea of each body paragraph. This sentence is called the *topic sentence*.

2 Identifying Relative Clauses

▶ Grammar Presentation

A relative clause modifies a noun and follows the noun it modifies. Identifying relative clauses provide necessary information about the noun. They are used in all kinds of academic writing, but they are especially useful in comparison and contrast writing to describe characteristics of elements that are being compared.

*Children **who / that have no siblings** are often very close to their parents.*
*People gradually behave in ways **which / that are more consistent with their preferred self-image**.*

2.1 Identifying Relative Clauses

a. An identifying relative clause modifies a noun. It begins with a relative pronoun: *that, which, who, whom,* or *whose*. (It is often called a *restrictive relative clause*.)

An identifying relative clause answers the question, "Which one?" It gives necessary information about the noun or noun phrase in the main clause. Without that information, the sentence would be incomplete.

IDENTIFYING RELATIVE CLAUSE
*People **who do not have children** may not be aware of differences in birth order.*
IDENTIFYING RELATIVE CLAUSE
*Creativity is a trait **that all middle children share**.*

b. *Who, that,* and *whom* refer to people. Use *whom* for object relative clauses. In informal speaking and writing, the use of *who* for *whom* is common.

PEOPLE
*Researchers **who / that study families** have different views.*
*My siblings are the people in my life **whom** I will always trust.*

4 Common Patterns That Show Contrast ◉

▶ Vocabulary Presentation

Useful words and phrases that show contrast in academic writing include *difference(s), differ, in contrast,* and *unlike*. These words are important in comparison and contrast writing.

*One **major difference** in some cultures is the role of adult children.*
***In contrast to** the past, more U.S. children now live with their parents into their early adulthood.*

4.1 Difference(s), Differ, In Contrast, Unlike

a. A common pattern with the noun *difference* is:

NOUN PHRASE
The difference between _____
NOUN PHRASE
and _____ is . . .

*One **significant difference between** youngest children **and** their older siblings **is** that youngest children receive a lot of attention.*

b. A common pattern with the verb *differ* is:

NOUN PHRASE   NOUN PHRASE
_____ differ(s) from _____ in that . . .

*The results of current research **differ from** earlier results **in that** they show a definite relationship between birth order and personality.*

c. Common expressions and patterns used with the phrase *in contrast* are:

NOUN PHRASE   INDEPENDENT CLAUSE
In contrast to _____, _____.

INDEPENDENT CLAUSE
In contrast, _____.

***In contrast to** traditional American families, the Chinese have had several generations of one-child families.*
*Many children without siblings receive a lot of attention. **In contrast**, children with siblings often share their parents' attention.*

d. A common pattern with the adjective *unlike* is:

NOUN PHRASE   INDEPENDENT CLAUSE
Unlike _____, _____.

***Unlike** firstborn children, youngest children are generally very creative.*

Data from the Real World, a feature unique to this series, takes students **beyond traditional information** and teaches them how the unit's **grammar and vocabulary** are used in authentic situations, including the differences between spoken and written use.

Students learn to *Avoid Common Mistakes* based on research in student writing.

2.2 Using Identifying Relative Clauses *(continued)*

b. Relative clauses are similar to subordinate clauses in that they are fragments if they appear alone.

FRAGMENT: *A recent study reports that firstborns are generally smarter than siblings. **Who are born later**.*

CORRECT: *A recent study reports that firstborns are generally smarter than siblings **who are born later**.*

Data from the Real World

| In academic writing, the relative pronoun **who** is more commonly used than **that** to refer to people. | Who | |
| | That | |

| In speaking, the relative pronoun **that** is more commonly used than **who** to refer to people. | Who | |
| | That | |

▶ **Grammar Application**

Exercise 2.1 Identifying Relative Clauses

A Read the paragraph about birth order. Complete each sentence with *that, who, whom,* or *whose*. Sometimes more than one answer is possible.

Birth order researchers have discovered some interesting information _that_ can help us understand
(1)
our colleagues better. Do you have a difficult boss
_____ authoritarian personality makes
(2)
your life difficult? If so, your boss might be a firstborn child.
Children _____ are born first are often
(3)
more authoritarian than their younger siblings. Do you
have a co-worker _____ is passive, but particularly creative and insightful?
(4)
This person may be a middle child. People _____ have both older and
(5)
younger siblings are often passive because their older siblings were responsible for their
well-being when they were young. The creativity _____ they exhibit might
(6)
be the effect of their having spent a lot of time on their own due to having to share parental
attention with their older and younger siblings. People _____ you work with
(7)

---

5 Avoid Common Mistakes ⚠️

1. Do not use *who* with inanimate nouns.
that
A study who showed the benefits of being an only child was published last year.

2. Do not omit the relative pronoun in subject relative clauses.
who
Children ˬhave older siblings tend to be somewhat dependent.

3. Remember that the subject and the verb must agree in relative clauses.
have
Children who has siblings often become secure and confident adults.

4. Use *the same as*, not *the same than*.
as
Middle children often have the same level of creativity than youngest children.

Editing Task

Find and correct eight more mistakes in this body paragraph from an essay comparing trends in families in the past and today.

Families Past and Present

A major way that families have changed is the number of families have only one child.
The number of families had only one child was low in the United States in the 1950s and
1960s. However, one-child families began increasing in the 1970s and are very common
today. This is especially true in households who have only one parent. One reason families
5 are smaller is the cost of living. It is not the same than it was 40 years ago. For example, it
costs about 10 times more to send a child to college than it did 40 years ago. As a result, many
parents choose to have only one child because they do not have enough money for more
children. In addition, attitudes about only children are also
not the same than attitudes about them in the past. In the
10 1950s and 1960s, people avoided having only one child. At
that time, many people thought that children did not have
siblings had many disadvantages. For example, people
thought that they did not learn good social skills. However,
recent studies who focus on only children show a different
15 picture. These studies show that only children tend to have
the same social skills than children who has siblings.

Theme-related exercises allow students to apply the grammar and vocabulary in a variety of natural contexts.

Next, students apply what they learn in **realistic editing tasks**.

The **Writing Process** section begins with presentation and practice of a **writing skill** and culminates in a *Writing Task*.

Before starting the **Writing Task**, students **organize and discuss their ideas.**

6 The Writing Process ✎

In this section, you will write an outline and one body paragraph for a comparison and contrast essay using the block method. Before you start writing, you will learn how to write effective topic sentences.

About Topic Sentences

Topic sentences introduce the main idea of a body paragraph. In academic essays, they often appear at the beginning of body paragraphs. Although not all body paragraphs have topic sentences, it will help you to organize your writing if you always include one.

The following guidelines will help you write effective topic sentences:

1. An effective topic sentence should contain a claim or an opinion that needs to be supported with evidence. It should not be a fact that is widely accepted as true. Notice the difference in the following sentences:
   - Some families are small. (a fact)
   - Small families are better than large families. (a claim that needs to be supported with evidence)

2. The content of the topic sentences should relate back to the thesis statement of the essay.
   - Siblings have different personality traits because of birth order. (thesis statement)
   - Firstborn children are generally leaders. (topic sentence)

3. The topic sentence is usually a general statement. It rarely contains detailed information. The details will come in the rest of the paragraph in sentences that convince the reader that the claim in the topic sentence is valid or true.
   - Middle children can be more solitary. (general statement)
   - Middle children do not always get a lot of attention. (detail to support the topic sentence)

4. Include words and phrases that connect one body paragraph to another.
   - *Unlike* middle children, those born last are often more easygoing.
   - *In addition to* being more easygoing, the youngest are also . . .
   - *Another* common trait of the youngest child is . . .

Organize Your Ideas

A For this assignment, you will use the block method of comparison and contrast for organizing your ideas.

Look at the block method outline for the essay on birth order below. Use the blank outline that follows to create an outline for your topic.

Title of Essay: Birth Order
Paragraph 1. Introductory paragraph. Thesis Statement: Experts agree that birth order tends to dictate some basic personality traits in children and adults.
Paragraph 2. Topic Sentence: Firstborn children often share several common traits. • Traits: responsible, ambitious, authoritarian
Paragraph 3. Topic Sentence: Middle children exhibit unique characteristics. • Traits: passive, solitary, realistic, creative, insightful
Paragraph 4. Topic Sentence: Youngest children have typical characteristics as well. • Traits: dependent, controlling, creative, easygoing, social

Title of Essay: _____
Paragraph 1. Introductory paragraph. Thesis Statement: _____
Paragraph 2. Topic Sentence: _____
• Details: _____
Paragraph 3. Topic Sentence: _____
• Details: _____
Paragraph 4. Topic Sentence: _____
• Details: _____

B *Pair Work* Share your outline with a partner and discuss your ideas.

Writing Task

Write one of the body paragraphs from your outline. Follow the steps below.

1. Make sure that you have a clear topic sentence that follows the guidelines in About Topic Sentences on page 76.
2. Include the following in your paragraph:
   - identifying relative clauses;
   - *as . . . as;*
   - common patterns that show contrast;
   - at least three of these academic words from the essay in this unit: *adulthood, assumed, author, benefit, creative, environment, exhibit, expert, indicate, individual, insightful, intelligent, maintain, passive, research, role, unique.*
3. After you write your paragraph, review it and make sure that you avoided the mistakes in the Avoid Common Mistakes chart on page 75.

Academic Writing Tip

Improving Your Internet Searches
When you do an Internet search, use quotation marks around important ideas. For example, "large families" will eliminate results with only "large" or "family" alone.

In the **Writing Task**, students **apply** the Unit's grammar, vocabulary, and writing skill.

Peer Review

A Exchange your outline and paragraph with a partner. Answer the following questions as you read your partner's outline and work, and share your responses.

1. Is the outline organized using the block method?
2. Does the topic sentence relate to the thesis statement?
3. Are any identifying relative clauses, *as . . . as,* or common patterns that show contrast used in the paragraph?
4. Is anything confusing? Write a question mark (?) next to it.
5. Provide one compliment (something you found interesting or unusual).

B Use your partner's comments to help you revise your paragraph. Use the Writer's Checklist on page A2 to review your paragraph for organization, grammar, and vocabulary.

Peer Review offers a structured way for students to give **constructive feedback** on each other's writing.

11

Classification and Definition 1: The Passive; Common Words and Phrases Used to Classify

Job Interviews

1 Grammar in the Real World

You will read an essay describing different types of job interviews. This essay is an example of a classification essay, which classifies information into groups or categories.

A *Before You Read* Have you ever gone on a job interview? What was the experience like? Read the essay. How does the writer classify different types of job interviews?

Job Interviews

Interviews are a familiar process for anyone entering the job market. They are by far the most common method used by companies to recruit new employees. All job interviews have the same goals – getting to know the job candidate better and giving the candidate a chance to learn about the job. However, they can take several different forms depending on geographic
5 location and format.

Depending on the geographic location of the candidates, interviews can be divided into two types: remote[1] and face-to-face. In remote interviews, candidates are geographically separated from the interviewers. This type of interview is usually the preferred method for initial screening,[2] as it eliminates traveling expenses. These interviews can be conducted over
10 a teleconferencing system or over the phone. Face-to-face interviews, in contrast, require the physical presence of the candidate. They are normally reserved for candidates who have already gone through a first round of remote screening.

Face-to-face interviews can be classified as either collective or sequential, depending on the number of people interacting with the candidate. Collective interviews can have two
15 possible structures: team interviews and group interviews. In a team interview, multiple interviewers interact with the candidate. In a group interview, multiple candidates are screened by a single interviewer. Sequential interviews, on the other hand, involve private, one-on-one conversations between the candidate and several interviewers, one after another.

As far as the format is concerned, interviews can be divided into two categories: structured
20 and unstructured. In a structured interview, the same list of questions is rigidly followed with all candidates. Companies sometimes use this format to ensure equal treatment among interviewees. It also makes it easy for recruiters to directly compare how two candidates responded to the

---

[1]**remote:** not near, at a distance, far away | [2]**screening:** the process of sorting something into different groups

same question. Conversely, unstructured interviews have a less strict format. Candidates might be asked more open-ended questions that encourage them to lead the discussion. For example,
25 the interviewer could start by asking candidates to talk about themselves. Interviewers could also ask them to describe their professional experience.

Finally, there are a few less conventional types of interview formats. One example is an audition. In this type of interview, recruiters might ask candidates to perform a task that simulates the actual duties of that job. For example, a candidate for a computer programming
30 position could be required to write a small piece of computer code. Candidates for a marketing job might be asked to persuade their interviewers to buy a fictitious product, and interviewees applying for a teaching job may be invited to prepare and deliver a mini-lesson.

Despite their possible variations, interviews should be seen as almost always having two main objectives. First, they are a way for the employer to test the potential employee. Second,
35 but equally important, they are an opportunity for candidates to learn more about the company and to evaluate their interest in the job. Being aware of the different types of interviews will help job seekers to be more prepared to accomplish those goals.

B Comprehension Check Answer the questions.

1. According to the writer, what are the main differences between remote and face-to-face interviews?
2. Why is an audition considered a less conventional type of interview?
3. Do you agree with the writer's conclusions in the final paragraph? Why or why not?

C Notice

1 **Classification and Definition Writing** Write the definitions of the terms below. Why is it important for the writer to define these terms?

1. Remote interviews _____
2. Face-to-face interviews _____
3. Collective interviews _____
4. Sequential interviews _____
5. Structured interviews _____
6. Unstructured interviews _____

2 **Grammar** Find sentences in the essay that mean the same as the sentences below and write the number of the line on which each sentence is located. Compare the underlined verbs below with the verbs in the sentences in the essay. What do you notice about the form of the verbs the writer used? Why do you think the writer uses this form?

1. It is possible to divide interviews into two types. _____
2. You can classify face-to-face interviews as either collective or sequential. _____
3. A single interviewer screens multiple candidates in a group interview. _____ .
4. Interviewers might ask a candidate for a marketing job to persuade them to buy a fictitious product. _____

3 **The Writing Process** Draw the chart below on a separate sheet of paper and complete it with the information from the essay.

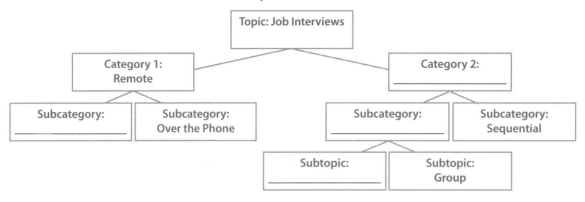

2 | The Passive

▶ Grammar Presentation

> The passive focuses on the action rather than the person or thing that receives the action. In academic writing, the passive can also improve text cohesion by making connections across sentences.
>
> *Candidates* ***are asked*** *several questions during the interview. The interview questions* ***are created*** *by a hiring committee.*

2.1 Forming the Passive

AGENT   OBJECT
The committee presented the results of the survey at the meeting. (Active).

The results of the survey were presented by the committee at the meeting (Passive).

2.2 The Passive

a. Passive and active sentences have similar meanings, but a different focus.

In active sentences, the subject is the agent – the person or thing that performs the action of the verb.

In passive sentences, the subject is the receiver – the person or thing that receives the action of the verb.

AGENT   RECEIVER
Active: *HR* ***screens*** *the candidates.*

RECEIVER   AGENT
Passive: *Candidates* ***are screened*** *by HR.*

2.2 The Passive *(continued)*

b. Passive sentences consist of a form of *be* and the past participle.

Simple present: *Remote interviews **are considered** to be effective.*

Present progressive: *The candidate **is being interviewed**.*

Present perfect: *The final candidates **have** already **been selected**.*

Simple past: *Candidates **were expected** to send a thank-you note after the interview.*

Past progressive: *The candidate **was being interviewed** when his cell phone rang.*

Past perfect: *Several candidates **had** already **been interviewed** when I arrived for my interview.*

c. The passive can also be used with modals.

*By Friday, several candidates **will have been chosen**.*

*Candidates **may be asked** difficult questions.*

*The candidates **should have been asked** more questions about their problem-solving skills.*

d. Some verbs that usually occur in the passive are followed by prepositions:

associated with, based on, compared to / with, involved in, linked to, related to

*Interview questions **should be based on** job requirements.*

e. The passive is often followed by infinitives with verbs for speaking and thinking.
   Common verbs are:

 ask, believe, expect, find, know, say, think, understand

*Approximately 100 people **are expected to apply** for the job.*

*Auditions **are known to be** effective job interview tools.*

Data from the Real World

The following verbs are commonly used in the passive in academic writing:

analyze, argue, carry out, conduct, consider, discuss, estimate, examine, explain, find, illustrate, include, note, observe, perform, present, study, suggest

*Personal questions about age and marital status **are** never **included** in the interview process.*

*Job responsibilities **are discussed** with the candidates at the interview.*

2.3 Using the Passive

a. Use the passive when the agent is not known, not obvious, or not important.

*Many types of interview formats **have been used** at the research lab.*

*Some candidates **are required** to perform a task.*

2.3 Using the Passive *(continued)*

b. Use the passive to improve the flow of ideas across sentences.	*In the group interview, multiple candidates **are screened** by a single interviewer. The interviewer asks a set of questions on standard topics. These questions **have been chosen** by the managers.*
c. Use the passive to describe a process. Common verbs are: *classify, compare, develop, examine, measure, study, test*	*In many community colleges, interview questions **are** carefully **developed** and **tested** before they are used. Face-to-face interviews **can be classified into** several different types.*
d. Use the passive to report news events.	*According to a government report, fewer people **were hired** by companies in June than in May.*

▶ Grammar Application

Exercise 2.1 The Passive

Rewrite the tips and information about job interviews by changing the parts of the sentence in bold from active to passive. Leave out the agent when it is not important, is unknown, or is obvious.

1. Occasionally **a member of the human resources staff will observe an interview**.

   Occasionally an interview will be observed by a member of the human resources staff.

2. **A company may not even consider you** for the job if you arrive late to the interview.

   _____

3. During the interview, **the interviewer will ask you questions** about your résumé.

   _____

4. **Interviewers may conduct interviews** over the phone.

   _____

5. One question you could ask is "What **training programs does the company offer**?"

   _____

6. **Employers often base the decision to employ someone on** a person's behavior during an interview.

   _____

7. **Federal and state laws prohibit employers** from asking certain questions about race, religion, and age.

   _____

8. **People have known some employers** to give tests during interviews.

   _____

9. If you do well, **an interviewer might ask you** to come in for a second interview.

_____

10. Interviewers often see more than one candidate in a day, so **they will probably compare you** with other candidates.

_____

Exercise 2.2 More on the Passive

A Complete the e-mail below about recent interviews at a software company. Use the correct passive form of the verbs and, where appropriate, modals in parentheses.

From: Peter Campbell

Date: October 14

To: Kim Chen

Subject: The search for project managers

Hi Kim,

Our search for new project managers is going very well so far. Ten interviews
have been conducted (conduct) this week so far. The following procedures
(1)
_____ (follow) each time. First, the interviewees all had individual interviews
(2)
during which they _____ (ask) about their previous work experience.
(3)
Then the interviewees _____ (divide) into two groups: those with project
(4)
management experience and those without that experience. After that, each interviewee
_____ (give) a problem-solving test. The test items _____
(5)   (6)
(base) on the kinds of problems that project managers might encounter. My experience has
shown me that a lot _____ (can / learn) about a candidate through
(7)
a problem-solving test.

Then the interviewees _____ (give) a short writing test. They
(8)
_____ (tell) when they applied that they might have to do some writing.
(9)
After the writing test, the interviewees went home. The tests _____
(10)
(should / evaluate) by Friday, and three interviewees _____ (will / choose)
(11)
to come in for second interviews.

Let me know if you have any questions.

Peter

B *Pair Work* Discuss with a partner your experiences or experiences of people you know with job or college interviews. Use the passive where possible.

When I went to the interview for my current job, I was interviewed by my manager first. Then I was asked to take a test. After that, they told me they would call me if they were interested. They called, and I went in, and I talked to someone in the personnel department.

3 Common Words and Phrases Used in Classification Writing 🌐

▶ Vocabulary Presentation

There are common words and phrases that writers use to organize or classify ideas in classification writing.

*Colleges **can be classified** into different types.*
*Most colleges offer the most popular majors, which **include** business administration and psychology.*

3.1 Classification Words and Phrases

a. Use the following common verbs and phrases (listed from most to least frequent) to classify ideas:

involves _____	*The job **involves** a lot of traveling.*
involves not only _____ but also _____	*Preparing for an interview **involves not only** physical preparation **but also** mental preparation.*
can be classified into _____	*Interviews **can be classified into** two types.*
is a combination of _____ , _____ , and _____	*A strong cover letter is **a combination of** confidence, preparation, **and** curiosity.*
consists of _____	*A typical job application **consists of** a cover letter and a résumé.*
is made up of _____	
can be / is / are divided into _____	*A résumé **is divided into** several key sections.*
is composed of _____	

b. Use the following common nouns to describe groupings:

categories, classifications, divisions, factions, groups, kinds, parts, sections, sets, types, units

*Job interviews can be divided into two **categories**.*
*Interviews can be divided into two **kinds**: remote and face-to-face.*
*There are two main **types** of interviews.*

3.1 Classification Words and Phrases *(continued)*

c. Use these common phrases to develop topics:

TOPIC, *which are* A *and* B.

TOPIC, *which include* A *and* B.

TOPIC, *such as* A *and* B.

TOPIC: A, B, *and* C.

TOPIC, *including* A, B, *and* C.

TOPIC. *These are* A, B, *and* C.

Notice the use of commas in these structures.

TOPIC
There are two main types of interviews,

A AND B
which are *remote* **and** *face-to-face.*

TOPIC
The field of health care provides many opportunities:

A B AND C
therapy, outpatient care, **and** *home health care.*

d. Use these common phrases to introduce the criterion (method) for classification: *according to, based on, depending on, on the basis of*

TOPIC   PHRASE
Job interviews can be classified **according to**

CRITERION
their structure.

PHRASE   CRITERION
Depending on *the number of participants,*

TOPIC
job interviews can be divided into two categories.

▶ Vocabulary Application

Exercise 3.1 Classification Words and Phrases

Choose the best word or words to complete the sentences about work.

1. A successful job search _____ determination, networking, and luck.
   a. can be divided into b. involves c. can be classified

2. Job descriptions on websites often _____ job titles, salaries, and benefits.
   a. are divided into b. can be classified into c. consist of

3. Succeeding in an interview _____ both preparation and an ability to adapt quickly to a situation.
   a. involves b. is composed of c. is made up of

4. Some companies prefer interviewing people in _____ .
   a. types b. parts c. groups

5. Most people want a job that _____ interesting opportunities, challenging tasks, and nice co-workers.
   a. is a combination of b. can be divided into c. can be classified into

6. Most businesses _____ several divisions.
   a. can be classified into   b. are composed of   c. involve

7. There are three _____ of a small business owner's job: managing employees, handling the finances, and marketing the business.
   a. kinds   b. sets   c. parts

8. Data Technician and Social Worker I are two _____ of government jobs listed online.
   a. classifications   b. sections   c. sets

Exercise 3.2 ◀)) More Classification Words and Phrases

Read the questions below. Then listen to a lecture about higher education in the United States. Take notes as you listen. Then write the answers to the questions in complete sentences. Use the classification nouns and phrases in parentheses in your answers.

1. How many categories can higher education in the United States be divided into?

   (can be divided) _Higher education in the United States can be divided into five categories, which are universities, community colleges, liberal arts colleges, vocational-technical and career colleges, and special interest colleges._

2. What are the main criteria for determining whether an institution of higher education is a community college or a university?

   (classified / according to) _____

   _____

3. What are the three degree programs in a university?

   (is composed of / generally) _____

   _____

4. What is another way that schools can be divided?

   (can be divided by) _____

   _____

5. How many funding classifications of schools are there?

   (which are) _____

   _____

6. What are the types of publicly supported schools?

   (can be subdivided into) _____

   _____

7. What are the advantages of attending a community college?

   (including) _____

   _____

Exercise 3.3 More Classification Words and Phrases

A Write sentences about job interviews using the words below and your own ideas.

1. a job interview involves

   I think a job interview involves not only talking about your experience but also making a good impression on the interviewers.

2. interviews can be classified into

   _____

3. a successful job search is a combination of

   _____

4. the perfect job involves

   _____

5. a good résumé consists of

   _____

6. I answer job advertisements on the basis of

   _____

B *Pair Work* Share your ideas with a partner. Decide which of your answers are the best. Report your best answers to the class.

I said that a job interview involves talking about your experience and making a good impression. My partner said that it involves finding out about job requirements. We agreed that my answer was probably the better answer because it's very competitive, so people need to sell themselves very well.

4 Avoid Common Mistakes ⚠

> **1. Remember to place the adverb after the modal in passive sentences.**
>
>   *often*
> Leadership skills can ˰ be ~~often~~ determined in group interviews.
>
> **2. Remember to use the correct preposition in the phrase *based on*.**
>
>   *on*
> The company's hiring decisions are based ~~in~~ candidates' interview behavior.
>
> **3. Remember to use the correct preposition in the phrase *involved in*.**
>
>   *in*
> The company vice presidents are rarely involved ~~on~~ hiring decisions.

Editing Task

Find and correct seven more mistakes in the introduction and body paragraph from an essay on ways to pay for a college education.

Funding Options for Higher Education

in

There are many issues involved ~~on~~ choosing an institution of higher education. A prospective student's choice might be based in the location of the institution, or it might be based in the reputation of the academic programs and the faculty. However, for many students, the process of choosing a university may be often determined by economics. A
5 college education may be one of the greatest expenditures an individual will make in his or her lifetime. If money is an issue in a student's choice, there are several funding options.

One funding option available to low-income college students is a grant. A grant is a sum of money that does not have to be paid back. Government programs are the primary source of education grants. In addition to government sources, grants may be sometimes
10 awarded by private organizations and companies. The main factor involved on the awarding of government grants is income level. Private grants may often be based in additional factors, such as ethnicity, grades, or other academic achievements. As reporting one's income is always involved on the process of applying for a grant, a good place to begin is with the U.S. Department of Education's Free Application for Federal Student Aid (FAFSA). The FAFSA
15 application simplifies the income reporting process and matches the applicant's income with several grant opportunities. Grants are often the first and best choice for students who cannot afford a college education on their own.

5 The Writing Process ✏

In this section, you will write an introductory paragraph and one body paragraph for a classification essay. Before you start writing, you will learn how to classify things into categories and subcategories.

About Classifying

When you are classifying ideas or things in an essay, it is important to identify the categories into which you are placing things. You should explain carefully what criteria you used as the basis for each category, so that you clearly differentiate one category from another. Often, as in the sample essay at the beginning of this chapter, you will further divide things into subcategories. Again, you should clearly show why the subdivision was necessary and what the differences are between the subcategories.

Your introductory paragraph should contain a thesis statement that states the categories that will be presented in the body of the essay.

Exercise

A In the box below are different ways to classify jobs. Match each classification type to one of the thesis statements below. Write the letter on the line.

> a. Jobs classified by the types of industries they are in
> b. Jobs classified by whether the salaries are low or high
> c. Jobs classified by what level of education is required

1. _____ New professions have developed in the past several decades; some of them require extensive educational training, while others require only a high school diploma.

2. _____ Explosive new growth in jobs can be divided into the areas of transportation, health care, and tourism.

3. _____ Perhaps not surprisingly, in some parts of the country, new jobs are available in two main areas: unskilled low-paying positions and high-risk positions in start-up companies that have the potential to be extremely well paying.

B *Pair Work* Classification writing contains elements of comparison and contrast writing. After identifying categories, academic writers often explain how the categories are different from or similar to each other. With a partner, explain how you might compare and contrast the different categories in each thesis statement in A.

Pre-writing Tasks

Choose a Topic

A Choose one of the topics below. You will write an introductory paragraph for this topic and one body paragraph.

- Types of majors
- Types of employers
- A topic of your own approved by your teacher

B *Pair Work* Share your chosen topic with a partner. Provide suggestions about ideas or facts to include. Make a list.

Organize Your Ideas

A Draw the chart below on a separate sheet of paper to help you organize your ideas. First, write the topic you chose in the top box. Then choose two of the ideas from your list and write them in the Category boxes. Write information about each of those categories in the subcategory boxes. Add more boxes if you need to.

B *Pair Work* Explain your chart to a partner. Ask your partner whether your categories are clear, and whether there are other ways you could divide your topic.

Writing Task

Write an introductory paragraph and a body paragraph for a classification and definition essay. Follow the steps below.

1. Using the information from your chart, write a thesis statement for the essay.

2. Include in the thesis statement the criteria you will use to classify your topic.

3. Write a hook that will work well for your topic.

4. Provide any necessary background information about the topic in the rest of the introductory paragraph.

5. In your body paragraph, discuss one of the categories mentioned in the thesis statement. Divide the category into its subcategories.

> **Academic Writing Tip**
>
> **Irregular Plurals in Academic Writing**
> Remember to use the correct plural forms of the following academic words: *appendix / appendices; criterion / criteria; fungus / fungi; hypothesis / hypotheses; phenomenon / phenomena; stimulus / stimuli.*

6. Include the following in your paragraphs:
   - the passive;
   - common words and phrases that can be used to classify;
   - at least three of these academic words from the essay in this unit: *aware, category, code, computer, conduct, contrast, conventional, definition, despite, eliminate, ensure, evaluate, finally, format, goal, initial, interact, involve, job, location, method, normally, physical, potential, process, professional, require, respond, rigidly, sequential, simulate, structure, task, team, topic, unstructured.*

7. After you write your paragraphs, review them and make sure you avoided the mistakes in the Avoid Common Mistakes chart on page 168.

Peer Review

A Exchange your paragraphs with a partner. Answer the following questions as you read your partner's paragraphs, and then share your responses.

1. Does the introductory paragraph introduce the topic and explain the criteria used to organize the topic? Do the criteria used relate well to the topic?

2. In the body paragraph, is one of the categories presented in the introductory paragraph described well?

3. Do the subcategories support the main category?

4. Has the writer used the passive in the essay? Is it used correctly?

5. What common words and phrases does the writer use to classify?

6. Is anything confusing? Write a question mark (?) next to it.

7. Provide one compliment (something you found interesting or unusual).

B Use your partner's comments to help you revise your paragraphs. Use the Writer's Checklist on page A2 to review your paragraphs for organization, grammar, and vocabulary.

12 Classification and Definition 2: The Language of Definition; Appositives

Your Ideal Job

1 Grammar in the Real World

You will read an essay that examines the theories of vocational psychologist John Holland. The essay is an example of classification and definition writing that shows how Holland categorizes people according to their personalities.

A *Before You Read* How would you describe your personality? Do you think that your personality influences your decision in careers? Read the essay. What are the six personality types?

Matching Personality Type and Work Environment

Most people spend over a third of their waking hours at work. Because work is such an enormous part of people's lives, their career choices are critical for personal and professional success. Vocational[1] counselors, who are trained to help with these choices, use many tools to help people find the best jobs. One tool is the use of personality tests to suggest job choices
5 that could lead to greater job satisfaction. The most popular of these tests was created by John Holland, a leading researcher in vocational psychology. He developed six categories of personality type – *Artistic, Investigative, Realistic, Social, Enterprising,* and *Conventional* – which are used to help identify the best job choices (Holland, 1997). Understanding these personality types can help identify an appropriate job for one's personality.

10   Each personality type has defining characteristics. An Artistic personality type refers to a person who enjoys creative activities like art, dance, or creative writing, and who generally avoids highly structured or repetitive activities. A person with an Investigative personality type, on the other hand, is defined as someone who likes to study and solve math or science problems. People who fall into the Investigative personality type generally see themselves as

[1]**vocational:** relating to a job, career, or profession

15 scientific and intellectual. Having a Realistic personality type means valuing practical work, such as jobs that require technical or manual skills and are productive. A person with a Realistic personality type particularly values environments where they produce goods or use machines. Other people have good skills at teaching, counseling, nursing, or giving information. They are referred to as Social personalities. People with Enterprising personalities are good at leading
20 people and selling things or ideas. Many entrepreneurs fall into the Enterprising category. Finally, people who have a Conventional personality type are able to work with written records and numbers in a systematic way. These people are usually very detail-oriented and value structure and planning.

Holland's personality types can provide insights into compatible jobs and work
25 environments where people can best use their abilities. For example, Realistic personality types would look for environments that allow them to use tools or machines and generally avoid those that require a lot of interaction with people. Artistic people are more likely to find satisfaction and success in an artistic environment, such as an arts center or theater. Someone with an Investigative personality type would be best suited for a job in an investigative
30 field, such as medicine or mathematics. Figure 1 provides examples of jobs that match each personality type. Holland believed that people who look for jobs that suit their abilities are more likely to find environments in which they can succeed and be satisfied.

Figure 1. Holland Personality Types and Career Examples

ARTISTIC	INVESTIGATIVE	REALISTIC	SOCIAL	ENTERPRISING	CONVENTIONAL
Architect	Mathematician	Auto Mechanic	Nurse	Flight Attendant	Accountant
Dancer	Professor	Cook	Teacher	Lawyer	Cashier
Musician	Scientist	Electrician	Therapist	Salesperson	Secretary

Matching someone's personality type with a work environment is actually a more complicated process because people are often a combination of two or three personality
35 types. This means that the range of suitable jobs can actually be quite diverse. For example, a person may have a Realistic personality type but also have characteristics of an Enterprising personality type and a Social personality type. This person would likely be suitable for a job as an electrician, a salesperson, or a nurse. Discovering one's major personality types involves using assessment tools that identify skills and strengths.

40 For many people, it is often a difficult task to decide on a career. Realizing that much of one's life will be spent doing a certain kind of work can make the decision stressful. Many people use tools like Holland's personality types to help make their decisions. Information about personality types can be interesting and useful. Holland's theory is a valuable guide for people in choosing satisfying jobs and careers.

B *Comprehension Check* Answer these questions.

1. Why are people's career choices so important for success?
2. According to the essay, how will understanding one's vocational personality type be helpful?
3. Based on this essay, what is your personality type? Why?

C Notice

1 Classification and Definition Writing In the chart below, write a definition of each personality type, based on information from the essay.

Personality type	Definition
1. Social	
2. Enterprising	
3. Realistic	

2 Grammar Find the sentences that contain the definitions of the personality types that follow to notice the grammar the writer uses to introduce the definitions. Underline the verb phrases used in each definition.

1. Artistic personality type on lines 10–12.
2. Investigative personality type on lines 12–14.
3. Realistic personality type on lines 15–16.
4. Social personality type on lines 18–19.

3 The Writing Process Complete the tasks below to notice how the writer creates cohesion by linking back to previous words and ideas in the essay using different ways:

1. Find *their* on line 2. Who does this pronoun refer to?
2. On lines 15–17 in the sentence beginning with "Having a Realistic personality . . . " the writer uses the word "valuing." In the sentence that follows, the writer uses a different form of the word to connect the ideas. What word does the writer use?
3. What pair of synonyms does the writer use in the sentences on lines 29–31? Why?

2 | The Language of Definition

▶ Grammar Presentation

> Definitions are very common in academic writing. Writers define key terms in the text so that readers will understand the exact meaning of the concepts being described. Definitions usually use the simple present form of *be*, the verb *means*, or the passive of certain verbs.
>
> *Having a Conventional personality type **means** being good at working with written records and numbers in a systematic way.*
> *A person with an Investigative personality type **is defined as** someone who likes to study and solve math or science problems.*

2.1 Definitions

a. A definition generally follows the pattern:

term + *be* + general noun + defining details

TERM   IS / ARE   GENERAL NOUN
Realistic personality types **are** *people*

DEFINING DETAILS
who value practical work.

A general noun names a larger category for the term being defined. It is more general than the term being defined.

DEFINED TERM   GENERAL NOUN
A Realistic person is a **person** *with practical skills.*
Visual learning means **learning** *by seeing.*

The defining details are often in the form of an identifying relative clause or a prepositional phrase.

IDENTIFYING RELATIVE CLAUSE
A headhunter is a person **whose job is to find qualified people to take high-paying jobs.**

PREPOSITIONAL PHRASE
A chief executive officer is the person **with the most important position in a company.**

---

b. You can also use the verb *mean* to define terms.

Conventional **means** *standard, predictable, or normal.*

---

c. Avoid gender-specific singular pronouns in definitions.

SINGULAR NOUN: GENDER-SPECIFIC
A general practitioner is a doctor who provides basic medical services to **his** *patients.* (This assumes the doctor is a man, not a woman.)

Make the noun plural and use *their.*

PLURAL NOUN: GENDER NEUTRAL
General practitioners are doctors who provide basic medical services to **their** *patients.*

OR

Keep the noun singular and use *his or her* or *his/her.*

SINGULAR NOUN: NEUTRAL
A general practitioner is a doctor who provides basic medical services to **his/her** *patients.*

2.2 The Passive in Definitions

You can use the verbs *call*, *define*, *know*, and *refer* in the passive when defining a term.
With *is/are defined as*, the definition comes last.
With *is/are known as*, *is/are called*, and *is/are referred to as*, the definition comes first.

TERM
A certified public accountant (CPA) **is defined as**

DEFINITION
a person who has passed a state accounting exam.

DEFINITION
A person who has passed a state accounting exam
TERM
is known as *a certified public accountant (CPA).*

DEFINITION
A person who instructs or trains others, especially in a
TERM
school, **is called** *a teacher.*

2.3 Using Definitions

a. Place the term being defined at the end of the sentence to make a stronger connection to the subject of the next sentence.	*People who are skillful at occupations such as nursing, teaching, and counseling are known as Social types.* *The types of people in this group like to work in social environments.* (The link between the term *Social types* and the next sentence is stronger.)
b. Break more complex definitions into two sentences. Use a pronoun in the second sentence to create cohesion.	*Some people are good at jobs that require working with numbers and following strict procedures.* ***They*** *are called Conventional personality types.* (The definition of *Conventional personality types* is in the previous sentence.)

▶ Grammar Application

Exercise 2.1 Identifying the Parts of Definitions

A Unscramble the sentences below and find definitions of different types of jobs.

1. who repairs / water pipes, baths, / is / a person / a plumber / and toilets

   A plumber is a person who repairs water pipes, baths, and toilets.

2. who designs / is a person / certain that they / new buildings and makes / an architect / are built correctly

   _____

3. sell merchandise / who work / are sometimes referred to / people / as sales associates / in stores and

   _____

4. is called / a musician / who / someone / is skilled / in playing music

   _____

5. out of materials / sculptors / make art / are artists / like clay, marble, and metal / who

   _____

6. as stylists / fashionable clothing, / who / hairstyles, and makeup / are known / people / help their clients choose

   _____

B Rewrite items 1–6 in Part A using the cues below.

1. (is called) _A person who repairs water pipes, baths, and toilets is called_
   a plumber.

2. (is referred to as) _____

   _____

3. (are people who) _____

   _____

4. (is defined as) _____

   _____

5. (are known as) _____

   _____

6. (are people who) _____

   _____

C *Pair Work* Think of definitions for other jobs. Ask questions and test your partner to see if he or she knows the name of the job. Use different defining language in your questions.

   A *What do you call someone who flies an airplane?*

   B *A person who flies an airplane is called a pilot.*

Exercise 2.2 Writing Definitions

A 🔊 Listen to two students who are studying for a criminal justice test. As you listen, match the terms with the correct definition.

Field	Noun	Noun	Verb	Verb	Adjective + Noun
law	testimony	bankruptcy	to appeal	to sentence	~~admissible evidence~~

1. _admissible evidence_ : the kind of evidence that juries or judges can consider in civil and criminal cases

2. _____ : a system of rules that a community recognizes as regulators of behaviors and actions of people

3. _____ : evidence presented orally by witnesses during trials or before grand juries

4. _____ : to ask a higher court to review a decision after a trial to determine if it was correct

5. _____ : to announce a punishment to someone convicted of a crime

6. _____ : a legal procedure for dealing with debt problems of individuals and businesses

B Write definitions for the terms in A using the verbs in parentheses.

1. (define) _Evidence that juries or judges can consider in civil and criminal_
   cases is defined as admissible evidence.

2. (be) _____

   _____

3. (know) _____

   _____

4. (means) _____

   _____

5. (call) _____

   _____

6. (refer) _____

   _____

3 | Appositives

▶ Grammar Presentation

To provide additional information about a noun or noun phrase in academic writing, you can use an appositive: a noun phrase that either defines, restates, or gives important additional information about the noun phrase it follows.

John Zappa, **president of Sylvania Community College***, believes that instructors should always be aware of different learning styles.*

People with Enterprising personalities, **personalities that have leadership traits***, are good at leading people and selling things or ideas.*

3.1 Appositives

a. An appositive is a noun phrase that refers to the same person or thing as the noun it follows.

A sentence with an appositive is similar in meaning to one with a nonidentifying relative clause. The only difference is the relative pronoun and *be* verb are left out.

MAIN NOUN   APPOSITIVE
John Holland, **a leading researcher in vocational psychology***, developed a theory about career choices.*
(*John Holland* and *a leading researcher* refer to the same person.)

NONIDENTIFYING RELATIVE CLAUSE
John Holland, **who is a leading researcher in vocational psychology***, developed a theory about career choices.*

3.1 **Appositives** *(continued)*

b. You usually set off an appositive with commas.

You can also use dashes or parentheses to set off an appositive.

MAIN NOUN   APPOSITIVE

*Enterprising personalities, **personalities that hold leadership traits**, are good at leading people and selling things or ideas.*

MAIN NOUN   APPOSITIVE

*Kinesthetic learners – **people who learn through moving, doing, and touching** – prefer actively exploring the physical world around them.*

MAIN NOUN

Workers with the Enterprising personality type

APPOSITIVE

***(people who are energetic, ambitious, and sociable)** often work in real estate agencies and law firms.*

c. You can also place an appositive before the noun that it refers to.

APPOSITIVE

***A leading vocational psychologist,** John Holland developed a well-known list of personality types.*

3.2 Using Appositives

a. You can use an appositive to provide a definition or description of a proper noun.

APPOSITIVE ADDING DESCRIPTION

*Ben Cohen, **co-founder of Ben & Jerry's Ice Cream**,*

APPOSITIVE PROVIDING A DEFINITION

*is a good example of a "Healer," **a business leader who provides nurturing harmony to a business**.*

b. You can use an appositive to refer to tables or figures and citations, or when you use an acronym (a word formed from the first letters or parts of other words) or an abbreviation.

References to tables and acronyms are usually in parentheses.

These uses are very common in academic writing.

To illustrate his theory, Holland created a model of

APPOSITIVE

*personality types **(Figure 1)**.*

Federal data are now collected using the North

APPOSITIVE

*American Industrial Classification System **(NAICS)**.*

▶ Grammar Application

Exercise 3.1 Appositives

The items below contain information about remarkable people and organizations. Rewrite each sentence or pair of sentences to make a sentence containing an appositive.

Michael Pollan   Bono   Howard Gardner

1. Michael Pollan is the author of *Food Rules* and *The Omnivore's Dilemma*. Michael Pollan believes we should all examine our eating habits.

    Michael Pollan, the author of Food Rules and The Omnivore's Dilemma, believes we should all examine our eating habits.

2. Steve Jobs, who was a driving force in technology, had an enormous impact on the way we use technology on a daily basis.

    _____

    _____

3. One supporter of the nonprofit housing organization Habitat for Humanity is Jimmy Carter. Jimmy Carter is a former U.S. president.

    _____

    _____

4. Desmond Tutu is a Nobel Peace Prize laureate and retired South African archbishop. Desmond Tutu has promoted peaceful conflict resolution for many years.

    _____

    _____

5. Dr. Douglas Schwartzentruber and Dr. Larry Kwak are cancer researchers. Dr. Douglas Schwartzentruber and Dr. Larry Kwak are both working separately to find a vaccine against cancer.

    _____

    _____

6. Bono is a famous singer with the band U2. Bono works to improve health and nutrition throughout the world.

_____

7. Howard Gardner proposed nine types of intelligences. The nine types of intelligences are in Table 1.

_____

_____

8. The Ronald McDonald House Charities help families of children who are receiving medical treatment for serious diseases. The abbreviation for the organization is RMHC.

_____

_____

Exercise 3.2 More Appositives

On a separate sheet of paper, write five sentences about people, places, or organizations that you know about, using appositives. Try to use different punctuation – commas, dashes, and parentheses – in your answers.

Jules Yakakao, an expert in English language learning, works at a major university in Côte d'Ivoire.

Human Rights Watch – an organization dedicated to defending human rights – is well respected.

4 Avoid Common Mistakes

1. **Remember to use singular and plural nouns correctly in definitions.**

   Artistic types are a person who enjoys creative activities.
   (people) (enjoy)

2. **Remember to use the correct verb form in the passive when giving definitions.**

   Sometimes, emergency medical technicians are refer to as paramedics.
   (referred)

3. **Remember to use the correct pronoun in relative clauses. Specifically, remember to use *who* only with animate nouns.**

   A résumé who does not include dates is called a functional résumé.
   (that)

   People which are energetic and sociable often work in sales.
   (who)

4. **Make sure your pronoun use is clear so that it can only refer to one preceding noun. Otherwise, use more precise words, not pronouns, to refer to previously mentioned nouns.**

   Julio and Luis are creative people. They work in an art studio making large murals. The murals are very expensive. Many people come to see them to learn about them.
   (the artists) (their work)

Editing Task

Find and correct seven more mistakes in the introduction and body paragraph from an essay about a personality test.

The Myers-Briggs Personality Type Indicator

The Myers-Briggs Type Indicator, MBTI, is a personality assessment tool ~~who~~ *that* has increasingly gained popularity in the workplace. It is based on a psychological theory developed by Carl Jung. Jung proposed that there are two basic categories of thinking styles: rational and irrational. Rational functions involve thinking and feeling. Irrational functions

5 involve sensing and intuition. Jung further proposed that there are two basic types of people, introverts and extroverts. While there are several personality qualities who psychologists associate with each type, introverts are usually define as people who are more interested in ideas and thinking. In contrast, extroverts are define as people who are more action-oriented. The MBTI has taken these four basic Jungian personality categories and types and established

10 four sets of opposing pairs: extrovert/introvert, sensing/intuition, thinking/feeling, and judgment/perception. While individuals use all of these thinking styles, their MBTI results indicate their thinking-style preferences. They can help match individuals to careers and help managers understand how to best work with these employees.

One of the MBTI personality types, ISTJ (Introvert, Sensing, Thinking, Judgment),

15 illustrates the way in which the MBTI assessment tool can match individuals to appropriate working environments. ISTJ personality types are a person who tends to be quiet. They prefer to be alone. They attend to details rather than to the Big Picture. They prefer thinking to feeling. This means that they use logic when making decisions. ISTJ personality types like controlled, organized environments. They are concrete, ordered, and

20 predictable. They are more in tune with facts than with other people's feelings. ISTJs do well as accountants and in law enforcement. Managers of ISTJ types who are having difficulty getting along with others need to take action. They can be placed in situations where they can work alone, for example. Other remedies for unhappy ISTJs might include moving them to a more organized work group.

5 | The Writing Process ✏

In this section, you will write an essay that will involve classifying topics and writing definitions of key terms. Before you start writing, you will learn how to use a variety of cohesive devices.

About Cohesive Devices

In academic writing, a writer often connects back to previously stated ideas or information. To help their readers see that connections are being made to these previously mentioned ideas and information, writers make use of several different devices, known collectively as *cohesive devices*. When writers use these devices, the text is more cohesive. This literally means it "sticks together" well.

Here are some different types of cohesive devices that you can use to make your writing more cohesive:

1. **Pronouns** refer back to previously mentioned nouns (e.g., *it, she, they*).
2. **Demonstratives** also refer back to previously mentioned nouns (e.g., *this, that, these, those*).
3. **Repetition of words and phrases** remind readers of what they have already read.
4. **Different word forms** of previously mentioned words also remind readers of what they have read (e.g., *resolve → resolution*).
5. **Synonyms** can also help create cohesion in a text by reminding readers of previously mentioned topics (e.g., *reduce → diminish*).
6. **Signal words and transitional expressions** clearly help readers see connections between different parts of a text (e.g., *so, because, then, for example*).

Exercise

Write the number of the cohesive device used above each word in bold.

1. Pronoun	2. Demonstrative	3. Repetition
4. Different word form	5. Synonym	6. Signal/Transitional word or phrase

According to Neil Fleming, a professor at Lincoln University, learning styles can be classified into several categories. Visual learners are defined as people who **learn** *(4)* through *(1)* seeing. **For this reason** **these** **learners** need to see the teacher's facial expressions to fully *(2)* *(3)* *(4)* understand the content of a lesson. **Students** who learn through listening are called Auditory *(5)* learners. **They** learn best through lectures and discussions. Finally, Kinesthetic **learners** refer *(6)* *(7)* to people who learn through moving, doing, and touching.

Pre-writing Task

Choose a Topic

A Howard Gardner is a psychologist who developed the theory of Multiple Intelligences. He divided intelligence into different categories that the brain uses in learning. Every individual uses these Intelligences in a unique way and often uses some Intelligences more than others. Read about Gardner's Multiple Intelligences.

Linguistic Intelligence is the ability to express your ideas and communicate well with other people through the use of language. Writers, lawyers, and others who value effective communication usually have linguistic intelligence.

Logical / Mathematical Intelligence is the ability to understand the principles and complex ideas of cause / effect systems, the way a scientist does, or to work well with numbers, the way a mathematician does.

Musical Rhythmic Intelligence is the ability to hear patterns in music, recognize them, and work with them. People with musical intelligence have music as a main part of their lives. In fact, some feel like life revolves around music.

Bodily / Kinesthetic Intelligence is the ability to be physical and use the body to solve problems or to perform in some way. Good examples are athletes, firefighters, and dancers.

Spatial Intelligence is the ability to understand space and where things are in relationship to each other – the way a sailor can navigate on the ocean, or the way a sculptor creates a work of art from a piece of stone or wood. Spatial intelligence can be either artistic or scientific.

Naturalist Intelligence is the ability to see differences in living things – plants and animals – and to be aware of the natural world around us, like geographical forms and climate. This ability was essential long ago when people were hunters; it is still important for people who work in fields like botany.

Intrapersonal Intelligence is the ability to honestly know yourself: your abilities and desires, likes and dislikes, and your reactions to different things. Many people like to be around these people who really seem to know themselves well.

Interpersonal Intelligence is being able to understand others. This ability is especially important for anybody who must deal with other people frequently, such as teachers, counselors, politicians, or people in sales.

Existential Intelligence is the ability to ask difficult questions about life, death, and spirituality.

Adapted from *Great performances online: Howard Gardner's multiple intelligences.* (n.d.) Used by permission of WNET New York Public Media. Retrieved from PBS online www.pbs.org

B *Pair Work* Discuss these questions with a partner:

1. Which Intelligences do you tend to use in learning? Give examples.

2. Think of people that you know and their jobs. What assumptions can you make about the types of Intelligences that are dominant?

3. What jobs might people with Existential and Intrapersonal Intelligences be good at?

C *Pair Work* Choose two types of Intelligences to write about in an essay. Explain to your partner why you chose them. Did you pick the same Intelligences?

Organize Your Ideas

A Use the chart below to organize information about the two types of Intelligences you chose. You may need to do some additional research in order to complete the chart.

Type of Intelligence		
Definition		
Skills		
People you know who have / don't have this type		
Suitable and unsuitable jobs		
Other characteristics		
Sources used in your research		

B *Pair Work* Share your chart with a partner who chose at least one different type of Intelligence. Help each other add to or modify the information in your charts.

Writing Task

Write a classification and definition essay about the two Intelligences you have chosen. Follow the steps below.

1. Using the information from your chart, write a thesis statement that previews what your essay is going to be about.

2. Write an introductory paragraph with a hook that introduces the topic and includes your thesis statement.

3. Write several body paragraphs that define your chosen intelligences and classify jobs and skills that work best with these Intelligences.

> **Academic Writing Tip**
>
> **Use Thought-Provoking Questions**
> Writers sometimes use thought-provoking questions in an introductory or concluding paragraph. For example:
> *How can students learn new information through ways that are unique to each individual?*

4. Write a concluding paragraph that restates the thesis statement and gives some suggestion or prediction for the future.

5. Include the following in your essay:
   - at least two definitions of key words and appositives to describe experts or writers from your sources;
   - a variety of cohesive devices to connect paragraphs as well as ideas within paragraphs;
   - at least three of these academic words from the essay in this unit: *appropriate, assessment, category, compatible, conventional, create, creative, define, definition, design, diverse, enormous, environment, finally, identify, insight, interaction, investigative, involve, job, major, oriented, process, professional, psychology, range, require, researcher, stressful, structure, task, technical, theory.*

6. After you write your essay, review it and make sure you avoided the mistakes in the Avoid Common Mistakes chart on page 181.

Peer Review

A Exchange your essay with a partner. Answer the following questions as you read your partner's essay, and then share your responses.

1. Does the introductory paragraph have a thesis statement that previews the content of the essay?

2. Does the rest of the essay match your expectations from reading the thesis statement? If not, explain.

3. Has the writer included any definitions? Put brackets around any definitions and underline any words or phrases used to introduce the definitions.

4. Has the writer used appositives? Has the writer used correct punctuation with the appositives?

5. Has the writer used any cohesive devices? Place a check mark (✓) next to three of them.

6. Is anything confusing? Write a question mark (?) next to it.

7. Provide one compliment (something you found interesting or unusual).

B Use your partner's comments to help you revise your essay. Use the Writer's Checklist on page A2 to review your essay for organization, grammar, and vocabulary.

13

Problem–Solution 1: Present Perfect and Present Perfect Progressive; Noun Phrase Structures

Food and Technology

1 Grammar in the Real World 🌐

You will read an essay about genetically modified food. The essay is an example of problem–solution writing, in which the writer poses a problem and then suggests some possible solutions.

A *Before You Read* Do you worry about the safety of the food you buy from supermarkets? What information do you think should be on the labels of packaged foods? Read the essay. What information does the writer want to see on food labels?

Genetically Modified Foods

Any time humans make technological advances, they have the potential to do great harm and great good. Genetically modified (GM) foods, which are foods that have had changes made to their DNA, are no exception. Many people believe that there are possible advantages to genetically modifying plants, for example, to improve their nutritional value or protect them
5 from pests as they grow. Recently, scientists have added a growth hormone to salmon for faster growth (DeNoon, 2010) and high starch to potatoes so that they absorb less oil when fried ("GM Crops: Costs and Benefits," n.d.). Despite these alleged[1] benefits, there are some scientists and consumer groups that fiercely question the safety of these foods for human consumption and the environment. Peter Katel (2010), a writer for CQ Researcher (a publication
10 that reports on congressional news) claims that more independent tests are needed in order to conclude whether GM foods are suitable for consumption by the general public. Researchers must continue to thoroughly test GM foods to verify their safety, and consumers need to educate themselves and demand that food companies be more open in their identification of food sources.

15 According to The Center for Food Safety, GM foods have entered nearly every sector of the food market (n.d.). This shift means that a majority of the public is consuming GM foods as part of their regular diet. Statistics detailed in 2010 by Patrick Byrne, a professor at Colorado State University, revealed a little known fact: From 60 to 70 percent of all prepared foods in a typical supermarket in the United States contain GM ingredients. However, little research
20 has been done concerning the existence of any short- or long-term side effects. Larry Trivieri, author of several books on alternative medicine, cites the fact that the U.S. Food and Drug Administration does not require independent safety tests on GM foods (2011). Because of the lack of conclusive research, Neal Barnard (2011), as well as other researchers, has been warning us that potential health risks may be associated with the consumption of these foods.

[1]**alleged:** said to be true, but without proof that it is true

25 As consumers, we must make informed choices in the food we buy for the sake of our families. To do that, we need to educate ourselves on the issues surrounding GM foods so that we can choose whether to buy this "enhanced" food or not. Even though research has been inconclusive as to the effects of eating GM foods, we have the right to know their presence in the food we buy. Currently, foods with genetically modified ingredients are not labeled as such. One way to address the problem is by systematically labeling foods. People have the right to
30 know what they are consuming. In 2001, Eli Kintisch, a writer for *The New Republic* (a well-known magazine of politics and arts), suggested that the few remaining products should be simply labeled "GM-free." Since then, some manufacturers have added these labels. Consumers should pressure food manufacturers to continue to add them.

35 More research on the effects of GM foods must be done promptly. People have already consumed a significant amount of these foods throughout the world, and that amount is increasing, yet there is concern that we do not understand the possible side effects on humans, other living things, and our environment. Consumers must educate themselves and make wise choices. While there
40 appear to be advantages to this technological advance, we must make sure that the good that GM foods do for society far outweighs any potential harm.

B *Comprehension Check* Answer the questions.

1. According to the writer, what is the problem with GM foods?
2. Give two reasons why food is genetically modified, according to the essay.
3. In the third paragraph, the word "enhanced" is in quotation marks. Why do you think the writer used quotation marks around this word?

C *Notice*

1 Problem–Solution Writing Look at the second paragraph, which states the problem. In that paragraph, the writer offers information from four different sources to convince the reader that GM foods may be a problem. Complete the chart below with the information described in each of the sources.

Source	Information
The Center for Food Safety	GM foods have entered nearly every sector of the food market. A majority of the public is consuming GM foods as part of their regular diet.
Patrick Byrne	
Larry Trivieri	
Neal Barnard	

2 Grammar Follow the instructions below to help you notice and understand how the writer uses the grammar to explain the problem.

1. Read the second paragraph again.
   a. Do the verbs *have entered* and *has been done* describe a period of time up to now or a specific time in the past?
   b. How does the meaning of the verb *has been warning* differ from the meaning of the verbs in a.? Which form of the verb emphasizes that the action is potentially still continuing, the present perfect or present perfect progressive?

2. Reread the sentence starting on line 17 beginning with "Statistics detailed in . . ." Why do you think the writer used the past form of the verb "reveal" (*revealed*) instead of the present perfect form (*has revealed*) in this sentence?

3 The Writing Process The writer uses the four strategies in the box below to try to convince the reader of the seriousness of the problem. Write the name of each strategy next to the sentence below that illustrates it.

| emotional appeal | fact | statistic | strong opinion |

1. People have a right to know what they are consuming. _____

2. The FDA does not require independent safety tests on GM foods. _____

3. From 60 to 70 percent of all prepared foods in supermarkets contain GM ingredients. _____

4. We must make informed choices in the food we buy for the sake of our families. _____

2 | Present Perfect and Present Perfect Progressive

▶ Grammar Presentation

In problem–solution writing, the present perfect is used to describe situations, recent research, or trends that have an impact on a problem. The present perfect emphasizes a time in the past up to now. The time period may or may not be completed but in both cases there is a connection to the present. The present perfect progressive describes an action that started in the past and emphasizes that it is still going on.

*Genetically modified food **has been** available in grocery stores for many years.*
*Researchers **have been studying** the impact of GM foods on our health.*

2.1 Using Present Perfect

a. Use the present perfect to describe an event that started at an unknown or unspecified time in the past. This event may be completed, or it may continue into the future. *Note:* Do not use the present perfect for events that happened at a specific time in the past.	*Some researchers* **demonstrated** *that genetically modified foods may cause damage to humans.* (completed event) *The consumption of GM foods* **has increased** *significantly in the last ten years.* (the event may continue) SIMPLE PAST *Sales of GM foods* **increased** *dramatically between 2001 and 2011.*
b. Use the present perfect to indicate that a past event relates to the present – it is still important *now*. These are often recent events. These events may include general experiences up to now.	*Researchers* **have discovered** *recently that some GM foods may not cause health problems.* (The discovery is important and relevant now.) *It is true that most people* **have not noticed** *any difference after eating GM foods.* *The research team* **has received** *several grants for GM food research.*
c. Use the present perfect to introduce general ideas and provide background information about a problem. Then use the simple past to fill in the details that led to the problem.	*The farming of GM foods* **has increased** *in recent years.* *In 2010, Brazil dramatically* **increased** *the use of land for farming GM crops.*
d. The adverbs *already, ever, never,* and *yet* often occur with the present perfect.	*Many farmers* **have already seen** *enormous gains in productivity using GM crops.* **Has** *any technological advance* **ever been accepted** *immediately?* *They* **haven't finished** *the research* **yet***.*
e. Use the present perfect in academic writing to refer to earlier parts of a text. You can also use the present perfect to refer to other research.	**As we have seen***, there is no easy answer to the problem of our nation's food shortage.* **Swanson (2010) has argued that** *labeling foods may be the only short-term solution to the problem of GM foods.* **Critics have examined** *the situation carefully but have not proposed any definitive solution to the problem.*

2.2 Using Present Perfect Progressive

a. Use the present perfect progressive to describe actions that started in the past and to emphasize that they continue to the present and may continue in the future. As with other progressive forms, do not use the present perfect progressive with stative verbs.	*Researchers* **have been warning** *us for many years that GM foods have potential health risks.* *This group* **has been studying** *the effects of GM foods since 2001.* (They are still studying them.) *Some scientists* **have believed** *for years that GM foods are unsafe.* NOT *Some scientists* ~~have been believing~~ *for years that GM foods are unsafe.*

2.2 Using Present Perfect Progressive *(continued)*

b. Use the present perfect progressive with time expressions to emphasize how long an action has been going on:

Use *all (semester), for (years), in (months), not . . . in (a long time)*, to show the duration of the action or event.

Use *since (2010)* to show the starting point of the action or event.

He**'s been collecting** data *all semester.*
They**'ve been interviewing** consumers *for three months.*
Stores **have not been carrying** that product *since 2010.*

c. The present perfect progressive often has no time expression associated with it.

What **has** your research group **been working on**?
We**'ve been studying** GM crops.

d. The present perfect and the present perfect progressive can often have the same meaning and can be used interchangeably.

The number of farms that grow GM foods **has increased** *since 2005.*
The number of farms that grow GM foods **has been increasing** *since 2005.*

▶ Grammar Application

Exercise 2.1 Present Perfect Forms or Simple Past?

A Complete the paragraph about one farmer's story about switching to organic farming. Use the passive where appropriate. Sometimes more than one answer is possible.

Since 1979, <u>*I've been farming*</u> (farm) using conventional methods and
          (1)

_____ (get) good results. However, after my first granddaughter
    (2)

_____ (be) born, I _____ (start) to think of the world that
    (3)   (4)

she would live in and to consider organic farming. It means making a lot of changes, though.

I _____ (always / apply) chemical fertilizers to promote plant growth, but
    (5)

that will change. For years, I _____ (spray) insecticides to reduce pests and
              (6)

disease, but that will change, too. Starting next year, I will use birds, insects, and traps to

do that. For the entire time I _____ (live) on the farm, chemical herbicides
           (7)

_____ (use) to kill weeds. Once in 1992, I _____ (use) natural
    (8)   (9)

herbicides, but they _____ (not work) well, so I _____ (stop)
          (10)   (11)

using them, and I _____ (go) back to using chemical herbicides. However,
       (12)

starting next year, I will rotate crops to manage weeds.

B *Pair Work* Role-play a discussion between two people with different views on genetically modified foods. Use the present perfect and present perfect progressive forms where appropriate.

Student A You are skeptical about the farming of GM foods and think that not enough research has been done. You do not trust food companies and you wish that more information about GM foods were available. You believe that the use of the foods may harm the ecosystem. Your solution: There should be more research done on GM foods.

Student B You are enthusiastic about GM foods. You have read some research on the foods and are convinced that they are not harmful and that our bodies will adapt to eating them. You think that the use of technology to create new foods will allow people to be healthier and potentially reduce starvation worldwide. Your solution: There should be more GM foods.

A *The farming of GM foods is a problem. The research on GM foods has suggested that they could be harmful, so I don't feel confident that the foods are good for society.*

B *I disagree. We've been eating these foods for years now with no ill effects, and it seems the advantages outweigh the disadvantages. . . .*

Exercise 2.2 More Present Perfect Forms or Simple Past?

Complete the sentences. Use the present perfect, present perfect progressive, or simple past of the verbs in parentheses. Use the passive forms when necessary. Circle any time markers that help you decide which form is correct. Sometimes more than one answer is possible.

1. From 2000 to 2007, the value of GM crops *increased* (increase) considerably.

2. For the past 20 years, researchers _____ (track) the areas used to grow GM crops in the world.

3. Over the past 15 years, the number of GM crops _____ (grow) significantly.

4. Over 309 million acres of land _____ (use) for GM crops in 2008 compared to 282 million in 2007.

5. Many people are not even aware that farmers _____ (begin) growing GM crops in the mid-nineties.

6. Statistics show that the global area of GM crops _____ (increase) steadily since the mid-nineties.

7. In 2010, farmers from 29 countries, including Brazil, Argentina, and India, _____ (plant) GM crops.

8. The effects of GM foods on people _____ (not / determine), and scientists continue to do research.

9. Research _____ (not / show) yet that GM foods have a negative effect on our health and environment.

10. Until there is definite proof that GM foods are not harmful, some people _____ (decide) to avoid them.

Source: Genetically modified plants: Global cultivation on 134 million hectares. (2010).
GMO Compass. Retrieved from www.gmo-compass.org

Exercise 2.3 🔊 More Present Perfect Forms and Simple Past

Read the statements below. Then listen to the radio program about urban gardening. As
you listen, decide if the statements are true or false. Circle *T* or *F*.

T/(F)   1. Residents of urban areas such as Los Angeles
grow vegetables in their apartment.

T / F   2. Mark Johnson started a rooftop garden five
years ago.

T / F   3. Mark Johnson no longer has a rooftop garden.

T / F   4. The neighborhood swap in Mark's neighborhood
started four years ago.

T / F   5. Emily Ling regularly brought cooked food to the
neighborhood swap.

T / F   6. Emily Ling goes every week to the neighborhood
swap.

T / F   7. Emily and her neighbors never buy vegetables from stores anymore.

T / F   8. Neighborhood gardens have been popular for a while in Emily's city.

T / F   9. Annie Suarez started to grow food in her local neighborhood garden in 2010.

T / F   10. Annie Suarez currently writes a gardening blog.

3 | Common Noun Phrase Structures 🌐

▶ Vocabulary Presentation

> In academic writing, certain noun phrase structures (sometimes called *shell nouns*) are
> used to identify and restate more complex ideas. They generally refer to information
> already mentioned or that will follow in the text. In problem–solution writing, these
> structures can be used to define a problem and explain its importance.
>
> *It is important to identify **the causes of** famine.*
>
> *Research needs to be done because of **the fact that** more and more people are consuming
> GM foods.*

3.1 Noun Phrases with *Of*

a. Some noun phrases with *of* explain, label, or define a concept. For example: *the basis of, the concept(s) of, the definition of, the essence of, the idea of, the meaning(s) of, the notion of*	*It is important that the public understands **the concept of** genetic engineering and its implications.* ***The definition of** organic farming is agriculture that relies on natural methods and limits the use of chemical fertilizers and pesticides.*

3.1 Noun Phrases with *Of* (continued)

b. Some noun phrases with *of* express consequences and outcomes. For example: *the cause(s) of, the consequence(s) of, the effect(s) of, the result(s) of*

*Consumers need to be aware of **the potential consequences of** GM foods on their health.*

*No one has studied **the effects** of GM foods on babies.*

c. Some noun phrases with *of* express goals. For example: *the aim of, the benefit(s) of, the goal(s) of, the purpose(s) of*

***The aim of** the program is to reduce reliance on pesticides.*

***The purpose of** food labeling is to help consumers make more informed decisions.*

d. Some noun phrases with *of* express the importance of a concept. For example: *the core of, the heart of, the importance of*

*Sustainability is **the heart of** organic farming.*

***The importance of** organic farming is sustainability – not harming the environment and managing it well.*

e. Some noun phrases with *of* indicate measure and quantity. For example:

the amount of, the frequency of, the majority of, a number of, the number of, the rest of

Note: A number of means "several" or "many" and is followed by the plural form of a verb. The number of refers to a specific number and is followed by the singular form of a verb.

*Consumers need to be aware of **the amount of** GM foods that they eat.*

***The majority of** GM products come from crops such as soybeans, corn, and cotton.*

***A number of** people **have asked** about the benefits of organic farming.*

***The number of** consumers who buy GM foods **is increasing**.*

3.2 Noun Phrases with *That* Clauses

a. Noun phrases with *that* clauses are used to:

express a fact: *conclusion, fact*

express an idea: *claim, idea, notion*

express a view: *belief, doubt, sense, view*

express a claim that is not yet proven: *assumption, hope, hypothesis, impression, observation, possibility, suggestion*

***The fact that** the population continues to increase makes efficient food production essential.*

*New research may support **the notion that** modifying food has a negative impact on health.*

*Many governments hold **the view that** genetically modified food has successfully fed many hungry people.*

*Many people are concerned about **the possibility that** GM foods can be dangerous.*

b. Noun phrases with *that* clauses can appear anywhere noun phrases appear (for example, as a subject or object).

SUBJECT
***The claim that GM foods can be beneficial** is true.*

SUBJECT
***The fact that conventional agricultural products can have an "organic" label** has created skepticism in consumers.*

OBJECT
*I support **the idea that GM foods should be labeled**.*

3.2 Noun Phrases with *That* Clauses *(continued)*

c. *The fact that* and *the idea that* are especially common expressions in academic writing.

The fact that often introduces ideas that are generally accepted. You can use *the fact that* to persuade. A reader is less likely to challenge a statement that follows *the fact that*. It suggests that the information is not an opinion.

The writer cites **the fact that** *no long-term studies have been done on the effects of GM foods.*

Not all consumers agree with **the idea that it is necessary to label foods**.

▶ Vocabulary Application

Exercise 3.1 Noun Phrases with *Of*

A Complete the sentences about genetically modified foods with an appropriate noun phrase from the box. Sometimes more than one answer is possible.

the aims of	the basis of	the benefits of	~~the concept of~~	the effects of
the heart of	the majority of	a number of	the number of	

1. _The concept of_ genetic modification is not new.

2. One of _____ modifying food genetically is to produce enough food, especially corn, rice, and soybeans, for people all over the world.

3. However, _____ genetic modification of food are still not completely understood.

4. In a recent study, _____ people surveyed were uncomfortable with the idea of GM foods. In fact, _____ them avoided the foods.

5. At _____ their concern is the fact that researchers don't really know whether GM foods are completely safe.

6. _____ GM foods produced every year is steadily growing.

7. Proponents of this technology talk about what _____ this technology will be; however, only time will tell if they are correct to be so optimistic.

8. Opponents of GM foods do not think that the government should allow more GM foods on _____ inconclusive findings.

B *Group Work* Work in a group to answer the questions about GM foods. Use the noun phrases from the word box in A in your answers. Then present your answers to the class.

1. What are some reasons why scientists created GM foods?

2. What are some advantages and disadvantages of GM foods?

3. What do you think the majority of people know about GM foods? What do they base their understandings on? What are some of their concerns?

Exercise 3.2 Noun Phrases with *That* Clauses

A Read about the benefits of eating locally grown food and circle the correct phrases to complete the sentences.

Among the many current food trends, one is based on (**the belief that**)/ **the fact that** it is better to (1) eat locally grown food than food exported from far away. **The doubt that / The notion that** local food is (2) better for you is based on a few facts.

First, **the idea that / the fact that** food has only (3) traveled a few miles to get to your supermarket means that the food is probably fresher than meat or produce that has been shipped from the other side of the world. There is **a conclusion that / possibility that** produce (4) that has traveled a long way may have lost some of its nutrients or begun to deteriorate during the trip.

Second, people who prefer local food might hold **the view that / the conclusion that** (5) eating locally grown food is good for the community. For example, buying this food supports local farmers and other food producers, like cheese manufacturers and bread bakers.

Third, **the doubt that / the hope that** eating locally grown food will help protect the (6) environment – because less fuel is required to transport the food – might motivate some people to follow this trend.

Ironically, locally grown food can sometimes be more expensive than exported food even though it doesn't have to travel very far. This is often due to **the impression that / the fact that** local food producers usually consist of small businesses (7) with high overhead costs and low levels of production.

B *Pair Work* What is your opinion of eating locally grown foods? What are the benefits? What are some possible disadvantages? Talk with a partner and explain your opinion. Use nouns phrases with *that*.

The possibility that exported food may be less nutritious is surprising to me. I didn't realize that food could lose nutritional value like that. I think the fact that locally grown food might be more nutritious is a strong argument for eating food that is produced near my home.

4 Avoid Common Mistakes ⚠

1. **Remember that noncount nouns such as *advice*, *equipment*, *evidence, information*, *knowledge*, and *research* do not have plural forms.**
   information
   We do not have enough ~~informations~~ on the health effects of GM foods.

2. **Remember to use *the fact that*, and not *this fact that*.**
   the
   Many people are not aware of ~~this~~ fact that many snack foods contain GM ingredients.

3. **Remember that a *number of* takes a plural count noun and plural verb.**
   experts agree
   A number of ~~expert agrees~~ that GM foods may help solve world hunger.

Editing Task

Find and correct eight more mistakes in the body paragraph from an essay on environmental problems associated with food production.

Engineered Food and the Environment

activists think
A number of animal rights ~~activist thinks~~ that laboratory-generated meat, also known
as cultured meat, provides a solution to the negative environmental effects of food production.
Cultured meat is grown in a laboratory from animal tissue cells. There are many benefits
of cultured meat. First, animals do not have to be killed for food. According to the animal
5 rights organization People for the Ethical Treatment of Animals (PETA), "More than 40 billion
chickens, fish, pigs, and cows are killed every year for food in the United States" (as cited in
Harder, 2008, para. 1). This fact that cultured meat would virtually eliminate animal suffering
is not in dispute. Additionally, most people are aware that raising animals for food is harmful
to the environment. This is because processing meat requires large amounts of resources such
10 as land and water. There is also a great deal of informations on this fact that raising animals for
meat contributes to greenhouse gases and pollutes water, air, and land. Recent researches on
the environmental impact of cultured meat is very promising. A number of environmentalist
agrees that cultured meat would greatly reduce greenhouse gas emissions. There is also
evidences that cultured meat might be healthier and safer. A number of scientist is continuing
15 to do researches on cultured meat. Many of these experts predict that we will see cultured meat
in supermarkets within five to ten years. It seems clear that relying more on engineered food
products may someday help to solve some of the environmental problems that we face today.

5 | The Writing Process ✒

In this section, you will write two paragraphs describing a problem and explaining its importance. Before you start writing, you will learn strategies for emphasizing the significance of a problem.

About Emphasizing the Significance of a Problem

When you are presenting a problem in problem–solution writing, it is important to use strong arguments and strong language to convince the reader that the problem is significant and worthy of discussion and analysis.

The following are strategies you can use to emphasize the significance of the problem:

1. **Use facts.**
   Sixty to seventy percent of all prepared foods in a typical supermarket in the United States contain GM ingredients and yet these foods are not labeled as such. Thus, a majority of the public are consuming these foods without their knowledge of it.

2. **Use examples.**
   For example, the FDA is considering the approval of genetically altered animals, such as cattle and pigs.

3. **Use strong opinions.**
   Unless we take immediate action now, it may well be too late to reverse what is happening.

4. **Use an emotional appeal.**
   We must ensure that our children and our grandchildren have a safe and healthy world to live in.

5. **Use statistics and, if possible, data from charts and graphs.**
   As shown in Figure 1, the percentage of planted acres of corn has risen significantly since 2005.

Figure 1

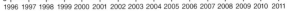

Growth in adoption of genetically engineered crops in the U.S.

Data for each crop category include varieties with both HT and Bt (stacked) traits.
Sources: 1996–1999 data are from Fernandez-Cornejo and McBride (2002). Data for 2000–11 are available in the ERS data product. Adoption of Genetically Engineered Crops in the U.S. tables 1–3

Exercise

A Write two arguments about each of the problems below, emphasizing the significance of the problem. In each sentence, use a different strategy.

1. As the world population grows, we need more and cheaper sources of food.

2. Foods that contain genetically modified organisms are not labeled in the United States.

3. The supply of fish worldwide is becoming depleted.

B *Pair Work* Share your arguments with a partner. Identify the strategies your partner uses – facts, statistics, emotional appeal, strong opinions.

Pre-writing Tasks

Choose a Topic

A Choose one of the topics below. You will write two paragraphs explaining the problem and giving two or three reasons for its significance.

- The demand for and the production costs of food are rising, while global population is increasing.

- The effects of climate change – increased frequency of droughts, floods, and extreme temperatures – have affected food production.

- A topic of your own approved by your teacher

B *Pair Work* Share your topic with a partner. Describe some of the reasons you believe the topic is significant. Give each other suggestions about reasons for the problem, why the problem is significant, and where to do research to find additional facts.

Organize Your Ideas

A Draw the chart below on a separate sheet of paper and complete it to organize your ideas. Describe the problem and write three reasons why the problem you chose is significant. If possible, give the source of your information.

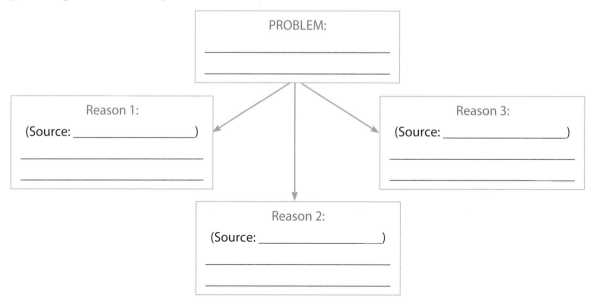

B *Group Work* In a small group, take turns presenting your ideas. Try to convince your classmates that your problem is more significant than theirs. After everyone has finished presenting, choose the most convincing presentation and explain why you chose that presentation.

Writing Task

Write two paragraphs that describe the problem and explain why the problem is significant using the ideas that you wrote in your chart. Follow the steps below.

1. Introduce and describe the problem, providing any historical or factual information that the reader may need to understand the background to the problem.

2. State two or three reasons why the problem is significant. Use strategies that you learned on page 199 to emphasize the significance of the problem.

3. Include the following in your paragraphs:

   • the present perfect and present perfect progressive to describe past situations that have an impact on present events;

   • noun phrases with *of* and *that* clauses;

   • at least three of these academic words from the essay in this unit: *alternative, benefits, challenging, cite, conclude, conclusive, consume, consumer, consumption, enhance, environment, identification, inconclusive, intensive, issue, label, labor, majority, modify, percent, potential, require, research, researcher, reveal, sector, shift, significant, source, statistics, technological.*

4. After you write your paragraphs, review them and make sure you avoided the mistakes in the Avoid Common Mistakes chart on page 198.

Peer Review

A Exchange your paragraph with a partner. Answer the following questions as you read your partner's paragraphs, and then share your responses.

1. Does the writer explain the problem clearly?

2. Do the paragraphs contain facts, statistics, opinions, and emotional appeals to convince the reader that the problem is significant?

3. Do the paragraphs include the present perfect and present perfect progressive? Underline any instances of these tenses.

4. Do the paragraphs include noun phrase structures with *of* and *that* clauses? Put brackets [ ] around any instances of these noun phrase structures.

5. Is anything confusing? Write a question mark (?) next to it.

6. Provide one compliment (something you found interesting or unusual).

B Use your partner's comments to help you revise your paragraphs. Use the Writer's Checklist on page A2 to review your paragraph for organization, grammar, and vocabulary.

Problem–Solution 2: Reporting Verbs; Adverb Clauses and Phrases with *As*; Vocabulary for Describing Information in Graphics

Children and Health

1 | Grammar in the Real World 🌐

You will read an essay that focuses on the problem of childhood obesity. The essay is an example of problem–solution writing, in which the writer describes the problem and the reasons why the problem exists. At the end of the essay, the writer voices a need to find a solution to the problem.

A *Before You Read* In what ways have the lifestyles of children changed in the past 20 years? How have these changes affected their health? Read the essay. According to the author, what are the main causes of childhood obesity?

Fighting Childhood Obesity

Childhood obesity is a major concern in the United States and in many other countries around the world. As shown in Figure 1, obesity in U.S. children has increased dramatically since the late 1980s. The Centers for Disease Control and Prevention (2011) state that an overweight or obese child has a Body Mass Index (BMI, a measure of weight in relation to the child's age,
5 sex, and height) above the 85th percentile for his or her age and sex. As an example of this, a second grader whose weight is above the 85th percentile would weigh 95 pounds or more. While it appears that the rates of obesity are falling for younger children, this trend is still likely to persist and perhaps worsen in the future for older children.

Former President Bill Clinton, a supporter of stronger policy on childhood obesity, asserts
10 that the causes of this health crisis range from overworked parents, with no time to prepare healthy food, to a lack of sidewalks and safe outside play areas for children (2010). Clinton also recognizes that a contributing factor is the marketing of inexpensive large-portion meals at fast-food restaurants. Companies make these meals for children even more attractive by giving away small toys and prizes with each meal.

15 Doctors are concerned about increased childhood obesity because of its health-related consequences. One consequence of obesity is cardiovascular disease.[1] Certain risk factors, such as high blood pressure, high cholesterol, and high blood sugar, are present in people who develop this disease. A study of obese children and adolescents has shown that approximately 60 percent of the participants had at least one risk factor for cardiovascular disease (A Change
20 of Pace Foundation, n.d.).

[1] **cardiovascular disease:** heart disease

There are additional health risks associated with being overweight or obese. Though less common, they are serious health issues. They include asthma, sleep apnea (when breathing stops during sleep for at least 10 seconds), and Type 2 diabetes. While Type 2 diabetes has been a common health consequence of adult obesity, in recent years it has become a problem among

25 children and adolescents (Bellows & Roach, 2011). Finally, other studies of obese children and teens have indicated that these young people are more likely to be obese when they are adults (American Academy of Child & Adolescent Psychiatry, 2011, para. 2).

Apart from physical issues, childhood obesity can also generate social problems. Puhl (2011) notes that overweight and obese children are often discriminated against socially, and that this

30 can cause stress and low self-esteem. These feelings are likely to have an impact on children's academic and social lives.

Figure 1.

Parents, doctors, scientists, and policy makers all believe that childhood obesity is a critical issue. It is clear that the reasons

35 for the rise in childhood obesity are complex. Therefore, the solution must involve everyone – parents, doctors, the media, as well as the community. A committed response now will ensure that the obese

40 child of today will not grow up to be an obese adult.

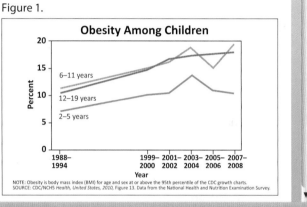

Obesity Among Children

NOTE: Obesity is body mass index (BMI) for age and sex at or above the 95th percentile of the CDC growth charts.
SOURCE: CDC/NCHS *Health, United States, 2010*, Figure 13. Data from the National Health and Nutrition Examination Survey.

B *Comprehension Check* Answer the questions.

1. According to the essay, what are some health issues that result from children being overweight or obese?

2. What are the social concerns for children who are overweight or obese?

3. Why does the author say, "It is clear that the reasons for the rise in childhood obesity are complex"?

C *Notice*

1 Problem–Solution Writing Notice how the writer not only states the problem, but also explores the reasons for and consequences of the problem. Draw the chart below on a separate sheet of paper and complete it with information from the essay.

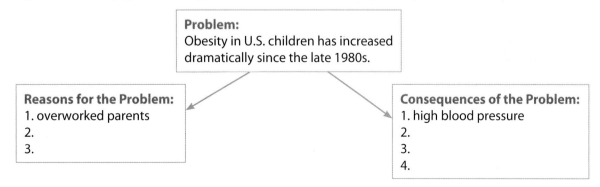

Problem:
Obesity in U.S. children has increased dramatically since the late 1980s.

Reasons for the Problem:
1. overworked parents
2.
3.

Consequences of the Problem:
1. high blood pressure
2.
3.
4.

2 Grammar Find the verbs that the writer uses to report ideas and information from sources. Write them on the blank lines.

1. The Centers for Disease Control and Prevention (2011) _state that_ ...

2. Former President Bill Clinton _____ ...

3. Finally, other studies of obese children and teens _____ ...

4. Puhl (2011) _____ ...

5. Parents, doctors, scientists, and policy makers all _____ ...

3 The Writing Process The writer of this essay brainstormed seven different reasons for childhood obesity; however, he or she chose not to include them all in the essay. Draw a line through the reasons that the writer did not include in the essay.

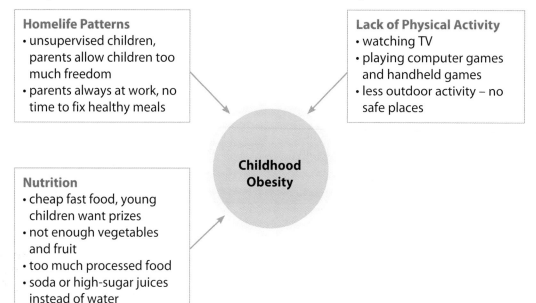

Homelife Patterns
• unsupervised children, parents allow children too much freedom
• parents always at work, no time to fix healthy meals

Lack of Physical Activity
• watching TV
• playing computer games and handheld games
• less outdoor activity – no safe places

Nutrition
• cheap fast food, young children want prizes
• not enough vegetables and fruit
• too much processed food
• soda or high-sugar juices instead of water

Childhood Obesity

2 | Reporting Verbs

▶ Grammar Presentation

Academic writers use reporting verbs to report ideas or findings from a source.

Bill Clinton (2010) **provides** *several reasons for the increase in childhood obesity.*
The study **illustrates** *several possible consequences of childhood obesity.*

2.1 Reporting Verbs

a. Reporting verbs have the pattern: the source + a reporting verb + *that* + clause with source's information.

SOURCE   REPORTING VERB
Puhl (2011) **points out that**
CLAUSE WITH SOURCE'S INFORMATION
obese children are targets of social discrimination.

b. In less formal writing, *that* can be omitted after a reporting verb.
It is better to keep *that* in academic writing.

INFORMAL: *Many parents **believe** children should avoid junk food.*
FORMAL: *Doctors **believe that** children should avoid junk food.*

c. Many reporting verbs, such as *illustrate, point out, show,* and *suggest,* can also be followed by a noun phrase.

NOUN PHRASE
*Figure 1 **illustrates** the three levels of influence on children's health.*

d. Some reporting verbs can only be followed by noun phrases and never by *that* clauses, for example:
describe, display, evaluate, give, investigate, present, summarize

*Chart 1 **describes** seven parental influences on children's health.*
NOT *Chart 1 describes* ~~that there are~~ *seven parental influences on children's health.*
*Figure 1 **gives** eight community influences on children's health.*

Data from the Real World

Common reporting verbs that take *that* clauses are (in order of frequency):

say, show, assume, suggest, complain, announce, argue, add, declare, explain, imply, mention, point out, propose, recommend, remark, report, state, write, warn

*A recent government report **suggests that** obesity is a problem for all ages, but it is most significant among children.*

2.2 Using Reporting Verbs

a. Most reporting verbs are neutral in tone. Use them to report facts.

*Research by Johnson (2009) **demonstrates that** the consumption of fast food has increased in the last 10 years.*
*The authors of the study **conclude that** childhood obesity can be very harmful.*

b. Use certain reporting verbs to report a point of view, for example:
believe, emphasize, predict, recognize, recommend, suggest

*The U.S. Department of Health and Human Services **believes that** people should read food labels carefully when shopping.*
*Doctors **recommend that** people get 30 minutes of exercise daily.*

c. Use certain reporting verbs to report results, for example:
conclude, demonstrate, estimate
Note: The verbs *demonstrate* and *estimate* can also be followed by a noun phrase, but the meaning is different.

*The U. S. Department of Health and Human Services **concluded that** consumers should read ingredient lists carefully.*
*The workshop **demonstrated** ways for children to improve their health.*

2.2 Using Reporting Verbs *(continued)*

d. Use *allege* and *claim* when you doubt or are unsure of the truth of the original author's statement.	*Ramirez (2007)* **claims that** *the number of fast-food restaurants in the world has increased.* *The attorney general* **alleges that** *the problem started with a complaint from parents in the public schools.*
e. Use *propose* and *suggest* when the author presents information as likely but still uncertain.	*Davidson (2010)* **suggests that** *the consumption of fast food has increased.*

▶ Grammar Application

Exercise 2.1 Reporting Verbs

Underline the reporting verbs in the letter to a newspaper about the problem of childhood obesity.

> Dear Editor,
>
> I want to bring your readers' attention to the issue of childhood obesity in the United
> States. Recent studies <u>show</u> that 32 percent of children and adolescents in the United
> States are overweight. Doctors claim that unhealthy childhood weight can affect adult
> weight. Some reports estimate that children who are overweight before the age of 15 are
> 5 80 percent more likely to be obese at 25 than children with healthy weights.
>
> Experts suggest that some of the main causes of childhood obesity are a lack of
> parental influences, a lack of nutritious foods available in the home, and availability
> of fast-food restaurants. However, we should also consider the role that school plays in
> influencing a child's diet and weight. Because students spend a large part of their day at
> 10 school, that is where they do much of their eating. Research indicates that children get
> about 40 percent of their daily calories while they are at school. This statistic suggests a
> link between school lunches and childhood obesity. In addition, most students these days
> have to do a lot of homework. Some parents estimate that their children have to do more
> than three hours of homework a night. This keeps them from spending their after-school
> 15 time engaging in physical activities. I don't want to blame schools for childhood obesity,
> but I do think we should all work together to help our children be healthy.
>
> Sincerely,
>
> A concerned parent

Exercise 2.2 More Reporting Verbs

A Complete the sentences with the appropriate reporting verbs. Remember to write *that* after the verb.

1. A report from the Dietary Guidelines for Americans (2005) _suggests that_ people should "eat fewer calories, be more active, and make wiser food choices" (p. vi).

   (a. suggest)   b. complain   c. demonstrates

2. The Centers for Disease Control and Prevention (CDC) _____ one way to fight childhood obesity is to remove high-calorie, low-nutrition snacks.

   a. emphasizes   b. illustrates   c. warns

3. Former President Bill Clinton (2010) _____ many parents are overworked and don't have time to prepare healthy food for their children.

   a. describes   b. believes   c. estimates

4. A report by the Centers for Disease Control and Prevention (2011) _____ a child whose body mass index is above the 85th percentile is overweight.

   a. states   b. recommends   c. warns

5. The Dietary Guidelines for Americans (2005) _____ people can reduce the risk of many chronic diseases, including cancer, through better nutrition.

   a. assumes   b. predicts   c. points out

6. A spokesperson from the American Academy of Pediatrics _____ it is unhealthy to allow children age two or younger to watch television.

   a. recommends   b. mentions   c. claims

7. The results of studies by Puhl (2011) _____ overweight children are often bullied and teased by their peers.

   a. evaluate   b. demonstrate   c. believe

8. Several states have had court cases in which the state _____ childhood obesity is a form of child abuse.

   a. has emphasized   b. has alleged   c. has recommended

B *Pair Work* Talk with a partner and explain your choices in A.

I think suggest *is the best answer for item 1 because the Dietary Guidelines are not forcing people to do anything, but telling people what might be a good thing for them to do. The guidelines are certainly not complaining about anything or demonstrating something.*

Exercise 2.3 Using Reporting Verbs

Pair Work Talk with a partner about one of the topics below or a topic approved by your teacher. Take notes on your partner's answers, and then report your partner's ideas to the class. Use reporting verbs in your report.

- At what age should children have cell phones?
- At what age should children be allowed to join social networks?
- At what age should children have their own computers?
- At what age should children have TVs in their rooms?

Monica argues that children under 10 should not have cell phones. She points out that cell phones are expensive and young children could easily break them. She also believes that children under 10 should always have an adult present, so they wouldn't need their own phones.

3 | Adverb Clauses and Phrases with As

▶ Grammar Presentation

Use adverb clauses and phrases with *as* to refer to a source of information.

***As seen in Figure 1**, the number of fast-food restaurants in the country has increased significantly.*

***As Smith and Jones (2005) point out**, there is a variety of reasons related to the increase in childhood obesity.*

3.1 Adverb Clauses and Phrases with *As*

a. Use adverb clauses with *as* to refer to information from a chart, graph, or other sources. Common verbs in *as* clauses are: *demonstrate, illustrate, point out, and show*	***As Figure 1 illustrates**, eating habits have changed recently.* ***As Puhl (2011) points out**, a key issue is the stigma of obesity.*
Use a comma after the clause.	***As Dr. Jarolimova illustrates,** there are many things that children can do every day to become healthier.*
b. You can also use adverb phrases with *as* in the passive, for example: *as demonstrated in / by _____, as illustrated in _____, as seen in _____,* and *as shown in / by _____*	***As demonstrated in Table 1**, there is a positive trend in the results.* ***As shown by Professor Green**, there are actions that can effectively address the problem.*
c. You can use the passive with modals, for example: *as can / may be seen in _____*	***As can be seen in Graph 1**, a higher percentage of boys has become overweight in the past several decades.*

▶ Grammar Application

Exercise 3.1 Using Adverb Clauses with As

A Answer the questions about the results of the Virginia Childhood Obesity Survey (2010). Use adverb clauses with *as* and the correct form of the verb in parentheses. Use the passive with modals where appropriate.

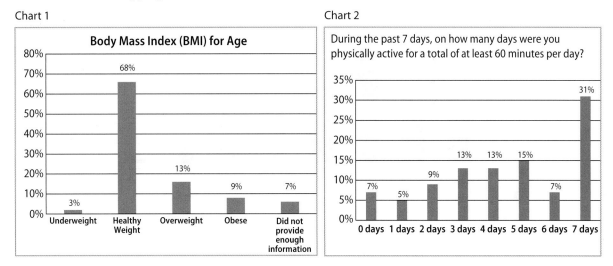

Chart 1

Body Mass Index (BMI) for Age

Chart 2

During the past 7 days, on how many days were you physically active for a total of at least 60 minutes per day?

1. What percentage of Virginia youth are physically active at least twice a week?

   (demonstrate) *As demonstrated in Chart 2, / As Chart 2 demonstrates, 88 percent of Virginia youth are physically active at least twice a week.*

2. What percentage of Virginia youth are obese?

   (show) _____

3. Are the majority of Virginia children overweight?

   (illustrate) _____

4. Are most Virginia youth active at least four days a week?

   (point out) _____

5. What percentage of Virginia youth are not at a healthy weight?

   (demonstrate)_____

6. What percentage of Virginia youth are physically active less than two days per week?

   (see) _____

B *Pair Work* Compare your answers with a partner. Then create two more questions and answers with the information in the chart.

Exercise 3.2 Using Adverb Phrases with As

Answer questions about the information from the Virginia Childhood Obesity Survey (2010).
Use adverb phrases with *as*.

Chart 3

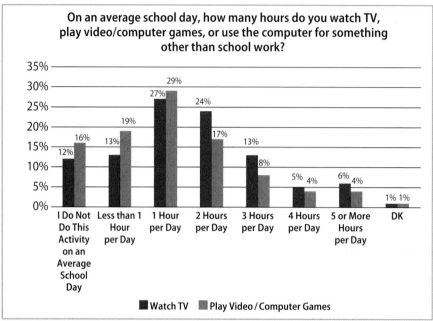

1. Compare the percentage of Virginia youth who watch TV for two or more hours per day
   with those who spend two or more hours playing video games.

   As Chart 3 shows, Virginia youth spend more time watching TV than
   playing video and computer games.

2. Compare the percentage of Virginia youth who don't watch TV with those who don't play
   video / computer games.

   _____

3. Compare the percentage of Virginia youth who spend one hour or less watching TV per day
   with those who spend one hour or less playing video / computer games.

   _____

4. Compare the percentage of Virginia youth who spend three hours per day playing video games
   with those who spend one hour playing video games.

   _____

5. Compare the percentage of Virginia youth who don't watch TV or play video / computer games
   with those who spend five or more hours watching TV and playing video / computer games.

   _____

4 Common Vocabulary for Describing Information in Graphics 🌐

▶ Vocabulary Presentation

Graphics (tables, charts, graphs) provide helpful visual support for ideas in writing. There are common words and phrases that are used to introduce the graphic and direct readers to specific information in it.

It can be seen from Figure 1 that *the number of girls and young women in sports has* *increased dramatically* *in recent decades.*

Chart 2 shows *that overall participation in physical education has* *declined.*

4.1 Common Vocabulary for Describing Information in Graphics

a. Refer to a graphic by first identifying it and then highlighting specific information that you want readers to notice. *Chart 1 shows* _____. *The graph shows (that)* _____.	IDENTIFY GRAPHIC HIGHLIGHT INFORMATION *Chart 1 shows that* *most students watched one hour or less of TV per average school day.* *The graph shows* *how many hours a day individuals from certain countries spend watching television.* *The graph shows that* *there is a relationship between weight and amount of exercise.*
b. You can use passive forms to identify a graphic. *From* _____, *it can be concluded / estimated / inferred / seen that* _____.	*From the chart,* *it can be concluded that* *individuals in the United States are getting much less exercise than a few decades ago.* *From the chart,* *it can be inferred that* *individuals in Switzerland maintain active lifestyles and healthy weights.*
c. You can use these nouns to describe change: ↑ *increase, rise* ↑↓ *fluctuation* ↓ *decline, decrease, drop, fall*	*There was* *an increase* *in girls' participation in team sports from 2002 to 2010.* *Figure 1 shows* *the fluctuation* *in funding for physical education in the last three decades.* *There was* *a decrease* *in students' participation in physical education between ninth grade and tenth grades.*

4.1 Common Vocabulary for Describing Information in Graphics *(continued)*

d. You can use the following adjectives to describe the intensity of a change:

slight, slow	*There was a **slight rise** in physical activity among ninth graders between 2007 and 2010.*
gradual, steady	*There was a **gradual decline** in physical education participation during high school.*
dramatic, rapid, sharp, steep, sudden	*There was a **sharp drop** in physical education participation between ninth and tenth grades.*

e. You can use the following verbs to describe a change: *decline, drop, fall, increase, reduce, rise*	*Participation in sports **fell** in three grades in the last few years.* *Participation **has increased** only for ninth graders.*

f. You can use the following verbs to indicate no change: *remain, stay, maintain*	*The hours students spent in physical activity each week has **remained** steady for the past few years.*

▶ # Vocabulary Application

Exercise 4.1 Vocabulary to Describe Chart Information

A ◀)) The principal at Cascades High School developed a program last year to address students' low energy levels. As you listen to the principal describe the program and its results, fill in the missing information in the line graph below.

Reports of Energy Levels

Very high
High
Moderate
Low
Very low

Sep   Oct   Nov   Dec   Jan   Feb   Mar   Apr   May

B *Pair Work*   Describe the information in the chart in A using the common vocabulary to describe chart information.

Exercise 4.2 More Vocabulary to Describe Chart Information

On a separate sheet of paper draw a chart similar to the one in Exercise 4.1. Imagine one year of reports of flu or colds among schoolchildren and create a line graph similar to the one in A. Describe your chart to a partner. Use the common vocabulary to describe charts.

As shown in the chart, the number of colds remained low from September through October. Then in November there was a sharp rise. This was probably a result of the fluctuation in temperature during the day and cold winds…

5 Avoid Common Mistakes ⚠

1. **Remember to use the base form of *be* after modals in the passive.**
   From the chart, it can ∧inferred that simple lifestyle changes result in major health gains. (be)

2. **Remember that reporting verbs such as *demonstrate*, *illustrate*, and *show* can be followed by a *that* clause or by a noun phrase. Be careful to use these two correctly.**
   Table C shows that ∧an increase in weight loss. (there is)
   Figure 8 illustrates ~~that~~ the results of increased exercise over a three-week period.

3. **In general, when referring to a numbered chart, graph, figure, or other source with *As . . .*, do not use an article.**
   As ~~the~~ Chart 1 shows, the number of hours participants engaged in physical activity per week had a direct effect on their body weight.

Editing Task

Find and correct eight more mistakes in the body paragraph from an essay on the problem of obesity.

Genetics and Obesity

Several studies have shown ~~that~~ a connection between genetics and obesity. As the Smith's 2009 study shows, people who have access to exactly the same foods will use those calories differently. Figure A demonstrates that the differences. It shows how a controlled diet and exercise program affected a group of 50 participants: some people in the group gained

5 weight, others maintained their weight, and a small percentage even lost weight. From this study, it can inferred that these different responses to the same situation are primarily genetic. Wu's research (2009) provides further support for the genetic connection to obesity. Her 2010 long-range study on body weight and family history clearly demonstrates that a genetic link to obesity. As the Figure B illustrates, there was very little variation in body weight among three

10 generations of ten families. Finally, several studies have shown that a connection between a gene called FTO and obesity. These studies also demonstrate that a relationship between FTO and diabetes and other diseases. From these and other studies, it can argued that genetics plays a role in body weight.

6 | The Writing Process ✏

In this section, you will write two paragraphs that give the reasons for and consequences of a problem. Before you start writing, you will learn how to narrow down a topic for an essay.

About Narrowing Down a Topic

As a writer, you probably have lots of ideas that you could include in your essay. However, part of your job as a writer is to narrow down the ideas to the few most important ones that you want to emphasize.

The following steps can help you decide what to emphasize:

1. **Brainstorm ideas.** Make a list of ideas about a topic.

2. **Narrow down the ideas.** Cross out ideas that are less important.

3. **Prioritize the ideas.** Put the remaining ideas in the order of importance.

Look at the chart below that a writer created for the topic "Factors at home that affect children's health." First, in column A she brainstormed the factors at home that can affect children's health. Next, in column B she narrowed down her ideas by crossing off three ideas that seemed less important. Finally, in column C she rearranged the remaining items in order of importance.

Topic: Factors at home that can affect children's health

A. Original Brainstorm List	B. Narrowed List	C. Prioritized List
Parents' knowledge about nutrition What parents actually eat Do parents encourage physical / outdoor activity? Kind of food available at home Parents' exercise and eating habits Parents' control of TV hours, video games	~~Parents' knowledge about nutrition~~ ~~What parents actually eat~~ Do parents encourage physical / outdoor activity? Kind of food available at home ~~Parents' exercise and eating habits~~ Parents' control of TV hours, video games	Kind of food available at home Parents' control of TV hours, video games Do parents encourage physical / outdoor activity?

Exercise

A *Pair Work* With a partner, brainstorm a list of factors that can affect children's performance at school. Use the chart above as a model. Then narrow the list down and prioritize the items.

Topic: Factors that can affect children's performance at school

A. Original Brainstorm List	B. Modified List	C. Prioritized List

B *Group Work* Compare your final list with other classmates and discuss your choices.

Pre-writing Tasks

Choose a Topic

A Choose one of the topics below. You will write two body paragraphs on your topic for a problem–solution essay. The first paragraph will explain the reasons for the problem, and the second paragraph will explain the consequences of the problem.

- The high dropout rate of U.S. high school students
- The drop in sports programs in high schools because of budget cuts
- A topic of your own approved by your teacher

B *Pair Work* Work with a partner to brainstorm a list of reasons for and the consequences of the problem. Then narrow down the topic. Finally, help each other search online for a table or chart that supports one or more of your ideas.

Organize Your Ideas

A Use the outline below to plan your paragraphs. Refer to your prioritized list of ideas. The topics of your body paragraphs should be in the same order as they appear in the list. Decide where to put the table or chart that you found that illustrates one of your points.

Topic:
Body paragraph 1: [the reasons for the problem]
Topic sentence:
Main points:
Body paragraph 2: [the consequences of the problem]
Topic sentence:
Main points:

B *Pair Work* Discuss your outline with a classmate and explain your choices.

Writing Task

Write two body paragraphs that belong in a problem–solution essay using the ideas in your outline above. Follow the steps below.

1. Write the first body paragraph focusing on the reasons for the problem.

2. Write the second body paragraph focusing on the consequences of the problem.

3. Use a chart or table in one of your paragraphs and refer to it.

4. Include the following:
   - appropriate reporting verbs;
   - adverb clauses with *as* and common vocabulary for describing graphics;

Academic Writing Tip

Citing Sources in Academic Writing
Academic institutions require writers to follow a certain style of writing. APA (American Psychological Association) and MLA (Modern Language Association) are common styles in academic writing. Student writers should ask their professors which style to follow.

- at least three of these academic words from the reading in this unit: *academic, adult, approximately, area, committed, community, complex, consequence, contribute, discriminate, dramatically, ensure, factor, generate, impact, indicate, involve, issue, major, media, normal, percent, persist, physical, policy, portion, range, response, stress, trend*

5. After you write your paragraphs, review them and make sure you avoided the mistakes in the Avoid Common Mistakes chart on page 213.

Peer Review

A Exchange your paragraphs with a partner. Answer the following questions as you read your partner's paragraphs, and then share your responses.

1. Has the writer included topic sentences in both paragraphs? Underline them.

2. What are the reasons for and consequences of the problem? Number them.

3. Is there a graph or chart that relates to the problem described in one of the paragraphs?

4. Are there any adverb clauses with *as* that refer to the graphic? Double underline them.

5. Are there reporting verbs? Circle them.

6. Is anything confusing? Write a question mark (?) next to it.

7. Provide one compliment (something you found interesting or unusual).

B Use your partner's comments to help you revise your paragraph. Use the Writer's Checklist on page A2 to review your paragraph for organization, grammar, and vocabulary.

Problem–Solution 3: Adverb Clauses and Infinitives of Purpose; Reduced Adverb Clauses; Vocabulary to Describe Problems and Solutions

Health and Technology

1 | Grammar in the Real World 🌐

You will read an essay about people who use the Internet to diagnose themselves and find information about illnesses. The essay is an example of problem–solution writing.

A *Before You Read* How often do you or people you know use the Internet to diagnose symptoms? Read the essay. According to the writer, what are some concerns that doctors have?

Patient–Doctor Relationships in the 21st Century

There was a time when a person with a medical problem would ask a family member, friend, or neighbor about their symptoms before visiting a doctor. Now, many people gather a great deal of information before their first visit. Their first source for this information is now the Internet. In fact, a survey by Pew Research Center's Internet & American Life Project (2011)
5 found that 80 percent of American adults use the Internet for health-related information. This increased use of the Internet for health purposes has led to a new phenomenon, *cyberchondria*. Cyberchondria is a situation in which people with no medical background diagnose themselves by reviewing symptoms and other information online and determine that their situation is worse than it really is. Educating patients about using online information,
10 identifying changes doctors could make, and using online medical information more effectively are all necessary in order to solve this problem of cyberchondria.

The term *cyberchondria* is based on the term *hypochondria*, a belief that one has a serious disease even though there is no medical confirmation. After gathering information online, cyberchondriacs often conclude that they have a disease or health issue that is worse than
15 the one that their doctor diagnoses (Torrey, 2009, para. 2). While not being a real physical condition, cyberchondria can lead to problems. For example, patients often find it difficult to accept their doctor's diagnosis, causing friction[1] between patients and doctors.

With patients self-diagnosing more often, a shift has occurred in the patient–doctor relationship. For example, patients may challenge doctors more aggressively and spend
20 more time discussing topics that they had researched online. Another concern is that patients do not always use credible websites. As a result, they may find information that is based on out-of-date research. Most importantly, doctors are concerned that patients will

[1]**friction:** unpleasant feelings caused by differences of opinion

scare themselves when reading symptoms online. As Brazilian cardiologist Dr. Fernando Botelho explains, "Patients read non-contextualized information and do not know how to process it.
25 This situation can bring anxiety" (personal communication, October 29, 2010).

While acknowledging these concerns, many doctors also see the benefit of having more actively engaged patients. Dr. Igor Barrios, a surgeon in Venezuela, believes that these changes will lead to better care. He feels that doctors will have to become more effective communicators (personal communication, October 29, 2010). Doctors should become more
30 sensitive to patients' more active role and learn to accept that they will have to be able to provide explanations for patients' questions about information they find on the Internet.

Using medical information available on the Internet wisely can also address the problem of cyberchondria. Health-care websites must state clearly that their information should be in addition to, rather than a replacement of, a consultation with a doctor and medical treatment.
35 For doctors, while it may be difficult, they need to acknowledge that the old rules have changed – they are no longer the only source of information. They should educate their patients on how to evaluate the health information they find on the Internet so that the process of diagnosing becomes collaborative rather than adversarial.[2] Finally, the last part of the solution involves patients. When searching for information on the Internet, patients should
40 remember that no website can replace a doctor's physical exam. Before approaching their doctor, they should check that the information they have is up-to-date and credible. In this way, they can avoid wasting time during appointments.

This cooperation will not be easy to implement. It will be difficult to persuade health-care website
45 providers to change information online. It will also be challenging for doctors and patients to change their roles, especially without additional training about these new relationships. However, when health-care website providers, doctors, and patients all realize that
50 these changes will benefit health care, they will be more likely to collaborate. This cooperation will help create a stronger twenty-first-century model for patient–doctor relationships.

[2]**adversarial:** opposing each other, like enemies

B Comprehension Check Answer the questions.

1. What is cyberchondria?

2. What concerns do doctors have when patients use the Internet to self-diagnose?

3. What is the solution suggested in the essay?

C Notice

1 Problem–Solution Writing Draw a chart like the one on page 220. Use the information in the essay to complete the chart, which shows that the proposed solution has three parts. Write the proposed solution for each part.

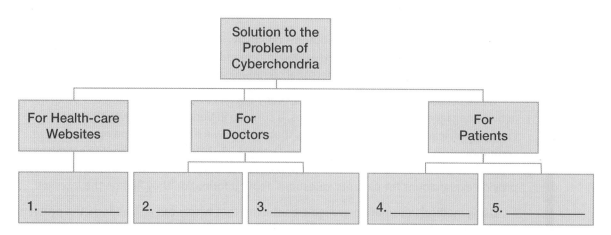

2 Grammar Follow the instructions below to notice how the author uses adverb clauses and phrases to express purpose or reason.

1. Find the last sentence in the first paragraph. Which phrase in the sentence explains the purpose of the parts of the solution.

2. Find the sentence that starts with *while* in the second paragraph. What form of the verb follows *while*? What is the understood subject of the phrase with *while*?

3. Find the sentences that contain *when* on lines 39–40 beginning with "When searching..." and on lines 48–51 beginning with "However, when health-care website providers..." How is the use of *when* in these two sentences different in structure?

3 The Writing Process What is the function of the concluding paragraph of the essay? Check (✓) all that apply.

_____ a) It restates the background to the problem.

_____ b) It summarizes the main parts of the solution.

_____ c) It considers problems that may arise from the solution.

_____ d) It suggests a couple of new solutions to the problem.

2 | Adverb Clauses of Purpose and Infinitives of Purpose

▶ Grammar Presentation

Adverb clauses of purpose and infinitives of purpose express the purpose, or reason, for an action or idea. They usually follow the main clause and are often used in problem–solution writing to explain the reasons for a proposed solution.

*Some clinics have computer stations **so that** patients can go online in the waiting room.*
*She researched the disease on the Internet **in order to** learn more about it.*

2.1 Adverb Clauses of Purpose

a. An adverb clause of purpose is a dependent clause that answers the question *why?*	*Doctors should educate their patients about how to evaluate medical information on the Internet **so that the process of diagnosing becomes collaborative rather than adversarial**.*
b. *So that* is the most common way to introduce clauses of purpose. Sometimes it is reduced to *so*.	*He cut down on fatty food **so that** he could lose weight.* *He cut down on fatty food **so** he could lose some weight.*
c. The adverb clause of purpose usually comes after the main clause.	COMMON: *The clinic provided training for using online medical reference information **so that patients would feel less anxious**.* LESS COMMON: ***So that patients would feel less anxious**, the doctors provided training for using online medical reference information.*

2.2 Infinitives of Purpose

a. When the subject of the main clause and the adverb clause of purpose are the same, you can use *in order* or *so as* with an infinitive (*to* + verb) of purpose. For example: *in order to* + verb You can omit the words *in order* when the meaning is clear. *so as to* + verb	*Doctors place brochures on medical conditions in their waiting rooms (**in order**) **to provide** patients with valuable information.* *Doctors should discuss treatment options with patients **so as to address** any concerns.*
b. You can also use these forms in the negative. The *not* comes before the infinitive: *in order not to* + verb *so as not to* + verb	*A patient might not say anything about what he or she reads on the Internet **in order not to make** the doctor angry.* *Patients should avoid the use of unqualified medical websites **so as not to make** false assumptions about their medical issues.*
c. When an infinitive is followed by an infinitive of purpose, you should use *in order to* or *so as to* for clarity.	UNCLEAR: *Some patients write a list of questions <u>to ask</u> **to use** time efficiently during medical appointments.* CLEAR: *Some patients write a list of questions <u>to ask</u> **in order to** use time efficiently during medical appointments.*

The 10 most common verbs that follow *in order to* are (in order of frequency):

be, make, get, obtain, keep, determine, avoid, see, protect, provide
*Why can't we e-mail our doctor **in order to make** an appointment?*

The 10 most common verbs that follow *so as to* are (in order of frequency):

avoid, be, make, provide, have, create, form, maintain, preserve, give
*Ari made his next appointment before he left the doctor's office **so as to avoid** having to do it later.*

▶ Grammar Application

Exercise 2.1 Adverb Clauses and Infinitives of Purpose

Read the magazine article about how a mother used the Internet to diagnose a disease. Underline seven more examples of adverb clauses and infinitives of purpose.

Before the invention of the Internet, people would visit their doctors in order to find out what was wrong with them. These days, when people begin to feel ill, they often turn to the Internet to diagnose themselves. Many medical professionals agree that self-diagnosis by the Internet can often cause unnecessary and unwarranted fears. However, once in a while, the
5 patient's hunches are correct.

Take the case of Alison Chambers. Alison has a 10-year-old son named Miles. When Miles was about two years old, he began getting fevers on a regular basis. She took him to a doctor to get help, and her doctor told her that children often get fevers and it was nothing to worry about. The doctor told Alison that Miles should stay home from day care when other children
10 were ill so as not to get sick. He also said that Miles should wash his hands often so that he would not pick up other children's germs as readily. Although Alison was very careful to follow the doctor's advice, Miles continued to get a fever about once a month. She took Miles to three more doctors so that she could get other opinions, but they all agreed with her doctor's diagnosis.

15 Alison began to get very frustrated and started researching Miles's symptoms online so as to find out some information for herself. She read about a rare disease whose symptoms sounded like Miles's symptoms. She visited Miles's doctor to ask his opinion. He thought it was unlikely that Miles had the disease, but he agreed to test him for it. The test showed that Miles did have the rare disease. Alison was scared but relieved to know what was wrong with her
20 son. Miles received treatment and stopped getting fevers soon after. It can be dangerous to rely on the Internet for medical information, but in Alison and Miles's case, it paid off.

Exercise 2.2 More Adverb Clauses and Infinitives of Purpose

A 🔊 Listen to the podcast interview about using digital tools for health. Then write answers to the questions using adverb clauses of purpose and infinitives of purpose.

1. Why did Cindy interview people?

   Cindy interviewed people to understand how they used digital tools to monitor and improve their health.

2. Why did a writer for the *New York Times* use Twitter?

   _____

   _____

3. Why does Pam use an app to take pictures of her food?

   _____

   _____

4. Why does Pam use a running app?

   _____

5. Why do people need to commit to using digital resources?

   _____

6. Why do we need to arrive at the doctor's office armed with knowledge?

   _____

7. Why might doctors have to change their relationships with patients?

   _____

8. Why does Jeff want Cindy to tell one more piece of advice?

   _____

B *Pair Work* With a partner discuss the apps that people used in the interview. Would they work for you? Why or why not? Which app seemed the most helpful to you? Why? What other apps have you heard about to improve health or break bad habits? What kind of app would you invent to improve your health and your life?

I liked the app that calculated calories based on pictures. I'd use it with my boyfriend so that I could persuade him to make better choices too. I don't run, but I'd like an app to motivate me and to remind me of my goals. I'd love someone to invent an app that I could easily use to describe symptoms and conditions in English so as to make it easier to communicate with doctors.

3 | Reducing Adverb Clauses to Phrases

▶ Grammar Presentation

> You can reduce adverb clauses to adverb phrases. The adverb phrase modifies the subject of the main clause. Adverb phrases can describe problems and solutions.
>
> *Sometimes patients become frightened **when they read symptoms online**.*
> → *Sometimes patients become frightened **when reading symptoms online.***

3.1 Adverb Phrases

a. You can reduce adverb clauses to phrases when they begin with *when*, *while*, *before*, and *after* and when the subject of the main clause and the adverb clause are the same.	ADVERB CLAUSE *Joanna tried various home remedies **before she saw the doctor**.* ADVERB PHRASE *Joanna tried various home remedies **before seeing the doctor**.*
b. If a clause contains a present progressive or past progressive verb, you can reduce the adverb clause by deleting the subject and the form of *be*.	***When I am dieting**, I never eat sugar or red meat.* ***When dieting**, I never eat sugar or red meat.* ***While Tran was searching** the Internet, he found positive reviews about his doctor.* ***While searching** the Internet, Tran found positive reviews about his doctor.*
c. If a clause contains a simple present or simple past verb, delete the subject and change the verb form to the *-ing* form.	***Before they see** a doctor, many patients use the Internet to find information about their symptoms.* ***Before seeing** a doctor for an appointment, many patients use the Internet to find information about their symptoms.* *In the past **before they saw** a doctor, people would ask for advice from family and friends.* *In the past **before seeing** a doctor, people would ask for advice from family and friends.*
d. If a clause contains a verb in the present perfect or past perfect, delete the subject of the adverb clause and change *have* or *had* to *having*.	***After you've read** multiple articles online, you'll have a better understanding of your doctor's diagnosis.* ***After having read** multiple articles online, you'll have a better understanding of your doctor's diagnosis.* ***After he'd read** multiple articles online, he had a better understanding of his doctor's diagnosis.* ***After having read** multiple articles online, he had a better understanding of his doctor's diagnosis.*

▶ Grammar Application

Exercise 3.1 Reducing Adverb Clauses

A Complete the excerpt from a blog entry for evaluating the information in health-related websites. Reduce each adverb clause to an adverb phrase. Remember to use commas.

A few months back I was plagued with headaches and fatigue.

Before going to the doctor, I decided to read up on possible diagnoses.
(1. before I went to the doctor)

_____ I was frantic. My long list of ailments included
(2. after I'd visited a few sites)

migraines, Lyme disease, and one deadly disease. _____
(3. while she was looking at the list)

my wife kept shaking her head and frowning. She asked me where I found the information.

I didn't remember. Then she e-mailed a friend of hers who is a nurse practitioner and we got

the following advice on how to use the Web wisely for research:

- _____ look for websites with the domains .gov and .edu,
(4. when you do research)
which tend to be more credible.

- Also, _____ look for websites that are operated by
(5. when you consider which websites to go to)
hospitals, universities, and recognized medical institutions.

- _____ search for the name of the author (if there is one)
(6. after you've read an article that interests you)
to find out his / her credentials.

- Be extra critical _____ . A lot of advertising might
(7. when you visit websites that try to sell you products)
mean that the objective of the website is really to sell merchandise.

- _____ make a list of questions about it to ask your
(8. after you collect all the information)
doctor.

- _____ if something doesn't feel right, you should tell
(9. after you've been diagnosed)
your doctor and continue your research because you never know when you'll come across

important new therapies and medicines for you and your doctor to discuss.

B _Pair Work_ With a partner, explain how you or someone you know uses the Internet for medical or health purposes. Use adverb phrases.

After hearing or reading about some new research on health that I'm interested in, I'll look it up on the Internet and find out more about it. While searching, I try to go to a variety of sites so that I can find out a few opinions of the information.

Exercise 3.2 Adverb Phrases

Combine each pair of sentences about online support groups. Use the appropriate adverb phrase with *when*, *while*, *before*, and *after*, depending on the sequence of the actions.

	First Action	Second Action	Simultaneous Actions
1.	Some people discover they have a serious illness.	Some people find help through online support groups.	
2.			• People go through treatment. • People find it comforting to communicate with others diagnosed with their disease.
3.	People talk with others about their illness.	People don't feel so alone.	
4.	People should read the messages that members post to make sure the group is supportive.	People choose a group to join.	
5.			• Leaders monitor members' messages. • Leaders should encourage positive participation.
6.	Members notice that a member is going through a difficult time.	The members of good groups offer encouragement and advice.	
7.	Members of good groups receive the support they asked for.	Members of good groups stay with the group and give others support.	

1. *After discovering they have an illness, some people find help through online support groups.*

2. _____

   _____

3. _____

   _____

4. _____

   _____

5. _____

   _____

6. _____

   _____

7. _____

   _____

4 | Common Vocabulary to Describe Problems and Solutions

▶ Vocabulary Presentation

> There are several common words and phrases that are useful in problem–solution writing.
>
> **The most important problem is** finding the right doctor to treat your illness.
> **There are several ways to address the problem of** cyberchondria.
> **One solution for** cyberchondria **would be to** avoid unreliable websites.

4.1 Phrases to Introduce Problems

Use the following phrases to introduce a problem:	
The key / main / primary / most important problem is _____ .	For doctors, **the main problem is** the extra time they spend arguing with ill-informed patients.
A / The secondary issue / problem is _____ .	**A secondary issue is** the patients' increased stress.
While _____ are issues / problems / factors, the most important / urgent / pressing / critical issue / problem is_____ .	**While** wasted time and patient stress **are factors, the most urgent issue is** misinformation on the Internet.

4.2 Phrases to Introduce Solutions

a. Use the following phrases to introduce solutions:	
The solution to the problem lies in _____ .	**The solution to the problem lies in** medical websites, doctors, and patients.
There are several ways to address the problem of _____ .	**There are several ways to address the problem of** cyberchondria.
One solution to / for _____ would be to _____ .	**One solution to** cyberchondria **would be to** educate patients.
The problem of _____ can be solved by _____ .	**The problem of** cyberchondria **can be solved by** reorganizing information on medical websites.
_____ is a possible solution to the problem of _____ .	Educating patients **is a possible solution to the problem of** cyberchondria.
b. Use the following phrases to make recommendations for possible solutions:	
is needed	A definite decision by the government **is needed**.
is necessary	Based on the results, it **will be necessary** to make changes to the treatment.
should be / may be / might be / must be considered	An individual's caloric needs **should be considered** before starting any diet.

▶ Vocabulary Application

Exercise 4.1 Phrases to Introduce Problems and Solutions

Complete the sentences about the patient–doctor relationship using phrases to introduce problems and solutions.

a secondary issue	one solution for the first problem	the problem of
can be solved by	~~the most important problem~~	

The most important problem when communicating with doctors
(1.)
is that sometimes they don't understand exactly what a patient is feeling.

_____ is the fact that patients don't always ask
(2.)
the right questions. _____ would be to require
(3.)
doctors to use checklists when discussing symptoms so that there is more discussion

of feelings. _____ asking the right questions
(4.)
_____ providing patients with frequently asked questions
(5.)
about their illness to help them come up with questions.

is necessary	there are several ways to address the problem of
the most urgent issue is	are issues
while	

The patient–doctor relationship has changed in recent years and new issues have arisen.

Patients come to appointments with a great deal of information and strong opinions. Doctors

can feel uncomfortable with their patients' new assertiveness, and patients can feel mistrustful

and even skeptical of their doctor's opinions. _____
(6.)
patients' mistrust and skepticism _____ ,
(7.)
_____ the antagonistic relationship that can develop.
(8.)
_____ antagonism. One way is for doctors to help their
(9.)
patients use the Internet more discerningly and discuss findings. In sum, a change in the

patient–doctor relationship _____ in order to adapt to the
(10.)
current information age.

Exercise 4.2 Phrases to Introduce Problems and Solutions

A *Pair Work* With a partner, rank the three problems below that doctors have with patients from 1 (the most serious) to 3 (the least serious).

- Some patients believe inaccurate information.
- Some patients don't follow advice.
- Some patients are unwilling to admit the seriousness of their health issues.

Next, decide on a possible solution for doctors to each problem. Use the phrases below or others in Chart 4.2 on page 227. Then share your ideas with another pair.

The primary issue with patients is . . .	*One solution to the problem might be . . .*
The secondary issue with patients is . . .	*. . . is a possible solution to the problem of . . .*
The last issue with patients is . . .	*The problem of . . . can be solved by . . .*

In my opinion, the primary issue with patients is that they don't follow their doctor's advice. I think that one solution to the problem might be for doctors to ask the patient to follow up and call after a week or two to report how he or she is doing. This will motivate the patient to follow the advice and avoid getting sicker.

B *Group Work* Work with a group and choose one of the problems concerning health issues below. Brainstorm possible solutions to the problem. Write one sentence describing the problem and three to four sentences describing possible solutions. Use the common phrases to introduce problems and solutions. Present your ideas to the class.

- You are sick and you disagree with your doctor's diagnosis.
- You have insomnia.
- You have a friend who is a cyberchondriac.
- A problem approved by your teacher.

There are many things you can do if you feel sick and you disagree with your doctor's diagnosis. One solution would be to . . .

5 | Avoid Common Mistakes ⚠️

1. **Remember that *for example* is always singular, even when several examples follow.**

   There are many solutions to the problem of cyberchondria. For ~~examples~~ *example*, using credible websites or avoiding the Internet altogether are ways to solve cyberchondria.

2. **Remember that the phrase *The problem of* is not followed by *the*.**

   The problem of ~~the~~ Internet addiction can be solved by limiting time spent online.

3. **Remember not to confuse *so that* (to express purpose) and *so* (to express result). Do not use a comma before *so that*.**

   The physician provided her patients with a list of credible medical ~~websites, so~~ *websites so that* they would stop arguing with her about their symptoms. *(purpose)*

   The patient stopped consulting medical ~~websites so that~~ *websites, so* he argued much less with his physician. *(result)*

Editing Task

Find and correct eight more mistakes in the body paragraph from an essay on the problem of cyberchondria.

Cyberchondria

A solution to the problem of ~~the~~ cyberchondria is to help individuals become informed Internet users. The Internet can be a useful source of information, but only if people use it wisely. Individuals need to know how to evaluate search results, so they can avoid misleading information. For examples, a website may be out of date, or it may not be published by a

5 credible medical source. Users should look for a date somewhere on the site, so they know that content is updated regularly. The solution to the problem of the unreliable medical websites is to establish the validity of sites. For examples, users should avoid sites with URLs ending in ".com" and sites that do not have scientific or medical sponsors. A commercial website that looks like a medical source may actually be a business selling products. However, medical sites

10 with URLs ending in ".gov" or ".edu" tend to have credible content so that users can be more confident of the information they contain. Physicians can also help solve the problem of the cyberchondria by directing their patients to their own preferred sites. This will reduce patient anxiety and frustration, so physicians can use their consultation time more productively.

6 The Writing Process ✒

In this section, you will write two paragraphs for a problem–solution essay. The paragraphs will include a solution to a problem and an evaluation of the solution. Before you start writing, you will learn different ways to evaluate a possible solution.

About Evaluating Proposed Solutions

When you propose one or more solutions to a problem, evaluate the solutions by mentioning any limitations. This will show the reader that you have considered the limitations and that despite any drawbacks to a solution, you still believe it is worth recommending. This will make your proposal stronger.

The following are ways to write about the limitations to a solution:

1. **The solution is not easy to implement.**
   The proposed solution will not be easy to implement because it will require changing longstanding habits and behavior. However, no important change happens overnight.

2. **The solution will not solve all aspects of the problem**.
   The proposed solution for addressing the problem of cyberchondria has some limitations. It will not completely prevent patients from consulting unreliable websites.

3. **The solution requires that certain conditions be met.**
   Before this solution is implemented, doctors need to accept the fact that they may no longer be the source of all the information.

4. **There are other solutions that can be beneficial.**
   Although this is not the only way to address the problem of Internet addiction, it is an effective way to obtain short-term results.

Exercise

A Match each solution to a limitation.

Possible Solution	Limitation
1. __e__ Hire more police.	a) A more attractive neighborhood may discourage vandalism, but it's not clear that it will lower other types of crime.
2. _____ Create neighborhood watch groups.	b) Monitoring the streets is a good start, but without a stronger police presence it will not be effective.
3. _____ Install video surveillance on dangerous streets.	c) Sports programs for bored teenagers are good. Other programs should be considered for them, too.
4. _____ Tidy up and beautify the neighborhood.	d) Neighbors will have to work together to create a schedule, and they have never been willing to work together.
5. _____ Provide afternoon sports programs for bored teenagers.	e) The cost of more officers on the street will not be possible without raising taxes or laying off other city employees.

B *Pair Work* Tell your answers to a partner. Identify each limitation as one of the four types in About Evaluating Proposed Solutions.

Hiring more police is a good solution. The problem is that this will mean that a city government will have to spend less money on some other city employees, like firefighters. This is limitation type 3: Certain conditions must be met.

Pre-writing Tasks

Choose a Topic

A Choose one of the topics listed below. You will write two paragraphs related to solutions for a problem–solution essay.

- People put off regular checkups at the doctor's office to save money.
- There is an increase in crime in your neighborhood.
- A topic of your own approved by your teacher

B *Pair Work* Share your topic with a partner. Brainstorm one or more solutions to your problem and then evaluate them. Think of possible limitations to your solutions.

Organize Your Ideas

A Do some research and reflect on your topic. Draw the chart below on a separate sheet of paper. Using the information from your research, complete your chart with possible solutions, supporting details, and any limitations to the solutions.

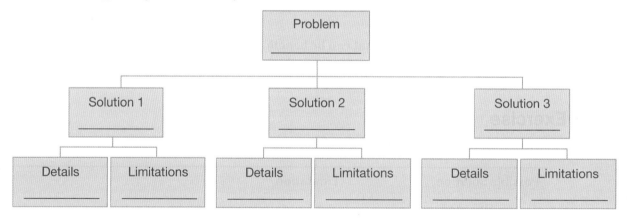

B *Pair Work* Share the information in your chart with a partner. Give each other suggestions about ideas or facts to include.

Writing Task

Write your two paragraphs for a problem–solution essay using your chart. Follow the steps below.

1. Choose one of the solutions in your chart and describe it in the first paragraph.

2. In the second paragraph, evaluate that solution and write about any limitations that it has.

3. Include the following in your paragraphs:

   - adverb clauses of purpose;

   - reduced adverb clauses with *when*, *while*, *before*, and *after*;

   - vocabulary that deals with problems and solutions;

   - at least three of these academic words from the essay in this unit: *acknowledge, adult, approach, available, benefit, challenge, challenging, communication, conclude, confirmation, consultation, contextualize, convince, cooperation, create, evaluate, identify, implement, involve, issue, medical, occur, percent, phenomenon, physical, process, research, role, shift, source, topics.*

4. After you write your paragraphs, review them and make sure you avoided the mistakes in the Avoid Common Mistakes chart on page 230.

> **Academic Writing Tip**
>
> **Use a Thesaurus to Build Your Vocabulary**
> A thesaurus can help you be more precise in your ideas, paraphrase ideas, and add variety to your writing.
>
> Doctors should ~~say that they don't know~~ *acknowledge that they* ~~everything.~~ *have limitations.*

Peer Review

A Exchange your paragraphs with a partner. Answer the following questions as you read your partner's paragraphs, and then share your responses.

1. Are there topic sentences in both paragraphs? Underline them.

2. Did the writer identify just one solution in the solution paragraph? What was it?

3. How many limitations were there in the second paragraph? Number them.

4. Does the writer use any adverb clauses of purpose or reduced adverb clauses? Underline any that you can find.

5. Does the writer use the vocabulary of problems and solution? Circle any words or phrases that you can find.

6. Is anything confusing? Write a question mark (?) next to it.

7. Provide one compliment (something you found interesting or unusual).

B Use your partner's comments to help you revise your paragraphs. Use the Writer's Checklist on page A2 to review your paragraphs for organization, grammar, and vocabulary.

Problem–Solution 4: *It* Constructions; Transition Words to Indicate Steps of a Solution

Leading a Healthy Life

1 | Grammar in the Real World 🌐

You will read an essay about changes that people can make in their lives in order to have a healthier lifestyle. In this problem–solution essay, the writer describes the process of implementing the solutions.

A *Before You Read* What are some things a person can do in order to live a healthy life? Why is it sometimes difficult in our modern world to do what is necessary to live a healthy life? Read the essay. What solutions to this problem does the writer suggest?

Leading a Healthy Life

In the last few decades, the average person's life has become increasingly unhealthy. The rules of modern society seem to have forced many into a stressful lifestyle. As individuals strive to meet the demands of their lives, they often overlook the multiple sources of stress and unhealthiness in their lives. Even though the task is challenging, it is not impossible to make
5 some changes that can lead to a healthier lifestyle.

Many factors can contribute to creating tension in everyday life. For most people, a busy work schedule usually prevents them from dedicating time to other stress-relieving activities. Lack of exercise and not enough sleep are only two of the consequences of such a lifestyle. Also, as time is consumed by work-related responsibilities, individuals tend to have less time to eat well. Many
10 people end up eating fast food as a strategy to save time, which adds to unhealthy practices.

Contrary to what many people may think, living a healthy life does not have to be difficult; nor does it have to be time-consuming. In terms of eating habits, a few changes can go a long way. First, individuals need to be committed to the challenge. Next, in order to have a healthier diet, they should buy low-calorie and low-fat foods that are easy to cook, such as
15 broccoli, cauliflower, carrots, chicken, and fish. Then they can cook more quantities of food over the weekend and freeze the leftovers in small containers so that the food can be consumed throughout the week. It has been argued that freezing the food destroys some of the nutrients. This may be true. However, this solution is certainly better than the fast-food option.

Just as with eating habits, it is a common belief that exercising takes away many hours of an
20 average person's week. However, first, it is important to find an activity that is enjoyable, such as playing a sport or hiking. Even simple activities, like taking the stairs, raking leaves, or

sweeping the floor, contribute to keeping someone active. Next, after finding an enjoyable activity, people need to commit to it. This means that people need to exercise regularly and make it part of their routine, just like brushing their teeth or combing their hair. Many people
25 will agree that their level of stress tends to decrease once exercising becomes part of their daily lives.

Maintaining a healthy lifestyle does not have to be challenging but can be accomplished with a series of small steps. Setting a few reachable goals can make a huge difference. Drastic diets, fasting,[1] or very demanding exercise routines are not that likely to generate permanent
30 improvements (as cited in Wong, 2010). On the contrary, it is essential to take a holistic approach[2] to good health. Such an approach starts with healthy food and regular exercise. When these items are part of someone's life, lack of time becomes just an excuse for not adopting a healthier lifestyle.

[1]**fasting:** intentionally eating no food for a long period of time | [2]**holistic approach:** a way of solving a health problem by looking at the social, psychological, and physical aspects of the problem

B *Comprehension Check* Answer the questions.

1. According to the essay, what is the main reason that people are prevented from leading a healthy life?
2. What are some of the beliefs that people have when it comes to healthy eating and exercising?
3. Do you think the writer would think that you have a healthy lifestyle? Why or why not?

C *Notice*

1 Problem–Solution Writing Reread the third and fourth paragraphs. Draw the chart and complete it with the missing information.

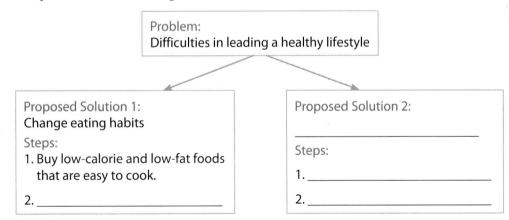

2 Grammar Follow the instructions below to help you notice how the writer uses *it* constructions:

1. Reread the sentence with the word *it* on lines 4–5 in the first paragraph and the sentence with the word *it* on lines 11–12. One *it* refers to a previously mentioned noun, but the other one doesn't. Which one doesn't refer to a previously mentioned noun?

2. Reread the sentence on line 17 with the word *it*. The writer uses the passive. Does the use of the passive and *it* make the sentence more subjective or objective?

3. Reread the sentence on lines 30–31 that begins with "On the contrary, . . . " Notice how the writer uses the word *it* to introduce his proposal. What adjective does the writer use after *it* to make the proposal stronger?

3 **The Writing Process** Label the different parts of the problem–solution essay in the margin of the essay. Note that each part may not be a whole paragraph.

- background information
- description of the problem
- solution
- steps of the solution
- limitations of the solution
- conclusion

2 | *It* Constructions

▶ Grammar Presentation

It constructions are commonly used in academic writing to make the text more impersonal and objective. In problem–solution writing, *it* constructions are often used when a solution to a problem is being proposed and evaluated.

It is important to *find an exercise that is enjoyable, such as playing a sport or hiking.*
It has been argued that *freezing the food destroys some of the nutrients.*

2.1 *It* Constructions

a. *It* constructions are formed in the following ways: *it* + *be* + adjective + *that* clause	**It is true that** *people who exercise usually have more energy than people who do not.*
it + *be* + adjective + infinitive *It* is not the subject. To provide a specific subject with infinitives, you can add *for* + noun phrase to the sentence.	**It is difficult to find** *time to exercise every day.* **It is difficult** <u>*for many adults*</u> **to find time** *to exercise every day.*
b. *Appear* and *seem* are verbs commonly used in *it* constructions. They are followed by a *that* clause: *it* + *appears / seems* + *that* clause *it* + *appears / seems* + adjective + *that* clause *Appear* and *seem* are used when the writer is almost certain, but not completely certain of the truth of the statement.	**It appears that** *researchers have made the connection between exercise and mental health.* **It seems that** *people who eat healthier are frequently in a good mood.* **It appears unlikely that** *the government will issue new guidelines for healthy eating within the year.*

2.1 *It* Constructions *(continued)*

c. You can use *it* constructions with a modal:
may, *might*, *could*
These modals soften claims that follow them.

> ***It may be true that*** *people who eat healthier are always in a good mood.*
>
> ***It might seem that*** *people are not losing weight when they start a new diet program.*
>
> ***It could be*** *that genetics plays the main role in obesity.*

Data from the Real World

Adjectives that frequently occur after *It is* to show evaluation are (in order of frequency):

important to, clear that, difficult to, possible that, possible to, necessary to, better to, impossible that, likely that, true that, essential to, common to, doubtful that, easy to, evident that, unlikely that
It is important to eat *a healthy diet and exercise every day.*

It seems is twice as common as *It appears*. Adjectives that frequently occur after *It seems* are:

likely, unlikely, clear, possible, reasonable, obvious, certain, impossible, logical, probable
It seems reasonable that *many people would make the connection between nutrition and physical health.*

Adjectives that frequently occur after *It appears* are:

possible, unlikely, plausible
It appears possible that *health insurance companies will provide more guidance on nutrition issues.*

2.2 *It* Constructions in the Passive

You can use *it* constructions in the passive with reporting verbs. This allows the writer to emphasize the idea without stating (or restating) the source.

> ***It has generally been accepted*** *that people who exercise frequently have more energy.*
>
> ***It was found*** *that certain fruits and vegetables can help with weight loss.*

Data from the Real World

Verbs that frequently occur in *it* + the passive form of the present perfect are:

shown, suggested, reported, proposed, demonstrated, determined, linked, observed, documented, called, estimated, used, recognized, known, found, argued, applied, approved, associated
It has been shown *that drastic diets are less likely to generate permanent health improvements.*

Modals that frequently occur with passive *it* constructions are:

can, should, could, and *must*
It can be argued that *schools should be more involved in teaching about healthy living.*
Note: Will, would, and *shall* are very infrequent in passive *it* constructions.

2.3 Using Adjectives in *It* Constructions

a. In problem–solution writing, certain adjectives can be used with *it* constructions to emphasize the importance of a problem and the effectiveness of the solution.

These adjectives include:

accepted, certain, clear, evident, important, indisputable, obvious

It is clear *that exercising is good for children.*

From the results of the study, **it is obvious** *that children are healthier if they watch only one hour of TV a day.*

---

b. Use the following adjectives to show the strength of the ideas or claims:

To show that something is certain, use *accepted, certain, indisputable,* or *true*.

To show that something is possible, use *likely* or *possible*.

To show that something is not likely, use *unlikely* or *unusual*.

To show that something is not possible, use *impossible*.

It is true *that children are heavier, but the causes are not clear.*

It is likely *that genes also play a big role in health.*

It appears unlikely *that cell phone use will decrease.*

It is impossible *to address health without including exercise.*

Use these adjectives to show the degree of difficulty:

difficult, easy, hard

It is difficult *to imagine restaurants eliminating desserts.*

Use these adjectives to show the writer's perspective:

clear, curious, evident, important, obvious, strange

It seems curious *that fruit and vegetables are not emphasized.*

It is evident *that people's lifestyles contribute to their stress.*

2.4 Using *It* Constructions

You can use an *it* construction instead of a statement that directly attributes the idea to someone.

Use *it* constructions as a more formal way of presenting information.

STATEMENT

Doctors and health officials agree that *people should exercise at least three times a week.*

IT CONSTRUCTION

It is important *to exercise at least three times a week.*

INFORMAL: **She argued that** *exercising is very time consuming.*

MORE FORMAL: **It has been argued** *that exercising is very time consuming.*

▶ Grammar Application

Exercise 2.1 *It* Constructions

A Choose the appropriate adjective to describe the idea in each sentence about health information. Then complete the new sentence with an *it* construction with the adjective. Use *that* or an infinitive. Use *for* and *not* where necessary.

1. People need to find time to prepare a healthy dinner every night.
   a. difficult   (b. important)   c. unusual

   It is important for people to find time to prepare a healthy dinner every night.

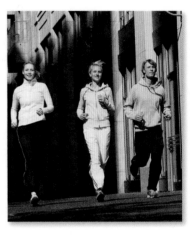

2. Everyone can eat good food by planning meals ahead of time.
   a. accepted   b. likely   c. easy

3. Young people don't usually pay attention to their dietary habits.
   a. possible   b. impossible   c. unusual

4. There is a good chance that meditation or yoga can reduce stress.
   a. possible   b. unlikely   c. obvious

5. Doctors agree that people should focus on their exercise and eating habits.
   a. clear   b. unlikely   c. strange

6. There is no doubt that moderate exercise results in fewer diseases such as diabetes.
   a. unlikely   b. indisputable   c. strange

7. There is a good chance that working out regularly improves mood.
   a. may be impossible   b. could be obvious   c. might be true

8. We can't really say why some people like to exercise and some don't.
   a. evident   b. impossible   c. reasonable

9. There is little evidence that regular exercise can cause physical harm.

   a. unlikely   b. impossible   c. important

___

10. Everyone knows that good support systems have a positive impact on one's health.

    a. curious   b. likely   c. evident

___

B *Pair Work* Think of four ideas that you have heard that have a positive or negative impact on health. Discuss them with a partner and give your opinion of the ideas. Then share them with another pair. Include statements that state something is certain, possible, not possible, or difficult.

From what we have read, it is accepted that vitamins can be beneficial for one's health. I personally don't think that people need vitamins if they eat well. I have also read that it appears unlikely that cell phone use is harmful to one's health. No one's really sure about this, though.

Exercise 2.2 Passive *It* Constructions

A Unscramble the sentences that compare medical beliefs today with medical beliefs in the past in the United States.

1. a. your health / accepted / cigarettes / bad for / it is / that / are

      It is accepted that cigarettes are bad for your health.

   b. the body / that tobacco / believed / was / it was / good for / in the 60s,

      ___

   c. thought / a person's life / and were good for / that cigarettes / might lengthen / years ago, / it was / his or her teeth

      ___

2. a. been recently / that sugar / one's health / it has / is bad for / shown

      ___

   b. a good source / argued / of energy for children / it was / that sugar was / years ago,

      ___

3. a. generally been / is bad for children / accepted / it has / that watching / too much television / now,

      ___

   b. suggested / that too much / it / from doing physical activities / has been / television keeps children

      ___

   c. children's grades / that watching television / could improve / it was / believed / in the 60s,

      ___

B *Group Work* As a group, compare medical beliefs of today with medical beliefs in the past. Share your ideas using passive *it* constructions.

It was once accepted that eggs were one of the causes of high cholesterol, but I think that it is evident from current research that they are not a primary cause.

3 Common Transition Words to Indicate Steps of a Solution

▶ Vocabulary Presentation

Transition words and phrases are commonly used to guide readers through the steps in a solution or process.

First, it is important for people to find an activity that is enjoyable, such as playing a sport or hiking. Next, they need to commit to doing it.

3.1 Using Transition Words to Indicate Steps of a Solution

a. Use transition words such as *first* and *to begin* to introduce the first step of a proposed solution. Use a comma after them when they appear at the beginning of the sentence.	*First, one needs to acknowledge that a problem exists.* *To begin, put the problem into words.*
b. Use *after that, following that, next, second, third, subsequently,* and *then* to introduce the next steps. Use *at the same time* to introduce a step that happens or needs to happen at the same time.	*Following that, ways to address specific aspects of the problem should be developed.* *Next, key terms should be clearly defined.* *At the same time, the scope and effects of the problem need to be identified.*
c. Use *finally, in the end, last,* and *lastly* to conclude the steps.	*Finally, the set of strategies should be implemented.*
d. You can also place transition words such as *next* and *then* in the middle of a sentence, before the verb. You can also use *next* at the end of a sentence.	*The scope and effects of the problem **then** need to be identified.* *The people associated with the problem need to be contacted **next**.*
e. You can also use phrases like *the first step, the second step, the third step,* and so forth, to indicate steps of a solution. These phrases are usually followed by *be* + infinitive.	*First, one needs to acknowledge that a problem exists.* *The first step is to acknowledge that a problem exists.*

3.2 Using Transition Words in Problem–Solution Writing

Use transition words to link the steps of a solution. This makes writing more cohesive.

First, one needs to acknowledge that a problem exists. The scope and effects of the problem **then** need to be identified. **Next**, key terms and ideas should be clearly defined. **Following that**, ways to address specific aspects of the problem should be developed. **Finally**, the set of strategies should be implemented.

▶ Vocabulary Application

Exercise 3.1 Transition Words to Indicate Steps of a Solution

A ◀)) Listen to part of a lecture about how companies can address specific health problems that occur on the job. Complete the steps of the solution, using the transition words you hear to identify the steps.

Notes:

Problem: For data-entry workers, sitting at a computer for hours every day leads to weight gain, back pain, neck pain, and wrist pain.

Solution: Set up a plan to address the specific problems that workers have.

Steps:

1. _____*The first step is to*_____ identify _____*the health issues*_____ .
2. _____ determine _____ .
3. _____ implement _____ .
4. _____ evaluate _____ .

B *Pair Work* Work with a partner and discuss one of the problems below. Using A as a model, write the problem, the solution, and possible steps for the solution. Include at least three transition words. When you have finished, report your problem and solutions to the class.

- Smokers who want to give up smoking
- Students who don't study enough
- People who worry too much

Exercise 3.2 More Transition Words to Indicate Steps of a Solution

Read the steps below about ways to make health a focus in your life. Number the sentences in the correct order.

_____ Next, keep a journal for a week and write down what you eat every day and how you spend your time.

_____ At the same time, substitute at least one hour of the time that you spent watching TV or doing some other unnecessary activity with one hour of exercise. Do this for 21 days because some experts claim that it takes 21 days to make or break a habit.

_1_ To begin, acknowledge that you need to focus on your health.

_____ Subsequently, look at your journal and circle the unhealthy foods that you ate during the week.

_____ At the same time, circle the things that you did during the week that were unnecessary or could be cut down. For example, did you spend your lunch break surfing online, or did you watch three hours of TV after dinner?

_____ Finally, evaluate how you feel after three weeks of eating better and exercising one hour a day. You should feel great and have more energy.

_____ Also, hopefully you'll have created a new, healthy habit for yourself!

_____ After you examine your journal, substitute each unhealthy food with a healthy food like fruit, vegetables, or lean proteins.

4 | Avoid Common Mistakes ⚠️

1. **Remember to use *It is important to* and not *It is import to* or *It is importand to*.**

   important
   It is ~~import~~ to admit that the problem exists.

   important
   It is ~~importand~~ to find an exercise routine that is convenient.

2. **Remember to use *to* or *for* after *impossible*.**

   to
   For many people, it is impossible ᶺfind the time for exercise.

   for
   It is impossible ᶺsome people to slow down and relax.

3. **Remember to use *then*, not *than*, when introducing next steps.**

   Then
   First, one needs to identify the sources of the stress. ~~Than~~, ways to eliminate them should be considered.

Editing Task

Find and correct six more mistakes in the body paragraph from an essay on ways to improve health.

important
It is ~~importand~~ to get an adequate amount of sleep in order to maintain a healthy lifestyle.

For many people, it is almost impossible get a good night's sleep. Stress and the demands of

work have a tremendous effect on one's ability to sleep. Lack of sleep can also result from certain

lifestyle habits. However, it is virtually impossible people to function well without adequate

5 sleep. Studies have shown that lack of sleep can lead to a variety of physical and emotional

problems. Therefore, it is import to get at least seven to eight hours of sleep at night because

getting the recommended amount of sleep means optimal health and energy, more acute

mental faculties, and a better memory. It also means getting sick less and being better able to

deal with the stresses and strains of everyday life. Although at times it may seem impossible get

10 enough sleep, there are a few simple strategies for improving one's chances. First, one needs to

determine the causes of sleeplessness, such as lack of exercise or consuming too much caffeine.

Than, one needs to commit to making a few small lifestyle changes. People who have difficulty

sleeping should increase their daily exercise, but not exercise too late in the day. They should

avoid consuming too much caffeine and eating close to bedtime. It is also important to have a

15 regular bedtime and to get the same number of hours of sleep each night. These small changes

to one's daily routine can lead to a better night's sleep and improved health.

5 The Writing Process ✏️

In this section, you will write a problem–solution essay in which you describe in detail how to implement the solution you propose. Before you start writing, you will learn about describing the steps of a solution.

About Describing the Steps of a Solution

When you describe a solution in problem–solution writing, it is important to develop a plan of action, or process, to implement the solution. All the steps involved in the planning and implementation of the solution should be explained.

The following guidelines can help you when writing about the steps in a solution:

1. **Reduce the steps to three or four major steps.** It can be very confusing for a reader to try to follow six, seven, or eight steps in a process. If you find that there are that many steps necessary to implement your solution, combine some steps into one so that your reader only perceives three or four, which should usually be the maximum.

2. **Use signal words or phrases.** To help your reader realize that you have finished writing about one step in the process and started writing about another, use transition words and phrases such as the following: *first; the first thing to do; second; next; after that; finally; the last step to take is . . .*

3. **Put the steps in a logical order.** Sometimes the steps in the solution will be in chronological order. In this case, it is obvious that you should write about the step that comes first in time, then second in time, and so on. In other cases, you may want to order the steps in order of importance. Often, this will mean writing about the most important step first. Later steps may be introduced by using such phrases as: *It is also important to . . .*

Exercise

A Read one student writer's solution to the problem of teenagers having a poor body image, and then answer the questions below.

An issue that is very important to young people is understanding and accepting their own bodies. Many young people, especially women, can develop unrealistic expectations about how they should look. This can cause a great deal of unhappiness and can lead to eating disorders and worse. Parents and teachers can take several practical steps to help young
5 people create a healthier sense of self. First, it is essential that parents and teachers learn about the warning signs of eating disorders and other body-image issues. When they have this information, they can act quickly and decisively to help young people who are in crisis. Next, parents and teachers should think about how they compliment girls. It is not unusual for girls to receive compliments only about their looks. Instead, parents and teachers should notice
10 what girls do, not how they look. Finally, parents and teachers should give young people a place where they can talk openly about how they feel when comparing themselves to thin girls or models they may see in fashion magazines. If young people realize that others have

similar feelings and issues, they may not feel alone. Young people are surrounded by media images of unrealistic body types that can make them feel insecure. However, following these
15 practical steps can help address avoidable suffering.

1. How many steps are there in the solution?

2. Did the writer use signal words to show where a new step begins? If so, what are they?

3. Are the steps organized in order of importance or in chronological order?

4. What are the steps described by the writer?

B *Pair Work* Discuss your answers with a partner.

Pre-writing Tasks

Choose a Topic

A Choose one of the topics listed below. You will write a problem–solution essay in which you propose at least one solution to your problem and describe the steps necessary to implement the solution. You will also note any limitations or drawbacks to your solutions and tell how you would address them.

- The park in your neighborhood is unsafe and unkempt. As a result, families don't use it for recreation and exercise.
- A social problem that is worldwide
- A topic of your own approved by your teacher

B *Pair Work* Share your topic with a partner. Then brainstorm some possible solutions to your problem.

Organize Your Ideas

A Draw the chart below on a separate sheet of paper. Write your problem, your suggested solution or solutions, the steps that need to be taken to implement your solution(s), and any limitations of your solution(s).

Problem:
_____

Proposed Solution 1:
_____

Steps:
1. _____
2. _____
3. _____

Limitation or Drawback to the Solution:
_____

How Will You Address It?
1. _____
2. _____

B *Pair Work* Share your chart with a partner. Discuss whether the steps to your solution(s) are logically ordered. Discuss the limitation you see and how you will address it. Does your partner agree?

Writing Task

Write a problem–solution essay in which you describe a problem and propose at least one solution and describe the steps necessary to implement the solution. Follow the steps below.

1. Write an introductory paragraph that describes the problem (including a hook) and includes the solution in your thesis statement.

2. In the second paragraph, explain the importance of the problem you chose.

3. In the next paragraph(s), propose a solution(s). Use the chart you filled out to guide you. Present the solution(s) and explain the steps necessary to implement each solution.

4. Acknowledge possible limitations or drawbacks to the solution(s) and how to address them.

> **Academic Writing Tip**
>
> **Keep an Error Log**
>
> Keep an error log with the mistakes you make and an explanation. Review the log as you write. For example:
>
> 1. ~~I think~~ it is important to eat healthily. (Avoid "*I think*" where possible.)
> 2. *It is*
>   ~~Is~~ essential for people to spend time relaxing. (Remember to include subjects.)

5. Write a concluding paragraph that restates your thesis statement and includes either a prediction or recommendation about your solution to the problem.

6. Include the following in your essay:

   • *it* constructions;

   • transition words and phrases that signal the different steps of a solution;

   • at least three of these academic words from the reading in this unit: *approach, challenge, challenging, cite, commit, committed, consequence, consume, contrary, contribute, create, decade, factor, generate, goal, individual, item, maintain, option, schedule, series, source, strategy, stress, stressful, task, tension.*

7. After you write your essay, review it and make sure you avoided the mistakes in the Avoid Common Mistakes chart on page 244.

Peer Review

A Exchange your essay with a partner. Answer the following questions as you read your partner's essay, and then share your responses.

1. Is there a thesis statement? Does it mention the solution to the problem?

2. Does the essay contain an effective description of the problem? What is the problem, and does the writer make the reader feel that it is important?

3. Does the essay contain a clear description of the steps necessary to implement the solution? Does it address any limitations or drawbacks to the solution? Does it consider other possible solutions?

4. Does the writer use any *it* constructions? Underline any that you find.

5. Does the writer use any transition words or phrases to signal steps in the process? Circle any that you find.

6. Is anything confusing? Write a question mark (?) next to it.

7. Provide one compliment (something you found interesting or unusual).

B Use your partner's comments to help you revise your essay. Use the Writer's Checklist on page A2 to review your essay for organization, grammar, and vocabulary.

17 Summary–Response: Past Unreal Conditionals; Phrases Used in Summary–Response Writing

Privacy in the Digital Age

1 Grammar in the Real World 🌐

You will read an article that discusses the issue of privacy and computers. You will then read an essay that summarizes and responds to the article.

A *Before You Read* What are some possible dangers of surfing the Internet? What can people do to protect themselves from these dangers? Read the article. Then read the response to the article below it. What do the two writers suggest as ways Internet users can protect themselves?

Privacy and Computers
by Robert Erani

In an era of online social media, people can announce any event to their virtual network of friends, family, and acquaintances within moments. From birthday celebrations to baby pictures, friends get news about each other from texts, tweets, or social networks. In addition, many people use credit cards to purchase products and complete numerous online forms with
5 personal information for a variety of purposes. As a result, personal information is ending up in the hands of other people. There are critics who are concerned by the lack of privacy. Despite such concerns, by following a few common-sense measures, people can use the Internet enjoyably and safely.

In our fast-paced world, social networking sites are, for many people, an important way to
10 keep up with friends and family. The issue now is how open one should be with sharing private information since the information could be stolen by criminals. For example, some people have had their homes broken into because they had posted the details of their vacation online. If they had not posted those details, the thieves would not have known that they had gone away. One way to reduce the risk of this happening is to activate the privacy controls on social
15 networking sites and smartphones. In other words, think about who will see your information and consider how they might use it.

Another important step is to shop only on secure websites so that one's accounts, passwords, and financial records are protected. Some experts recommend that people should treat their online information like they would treat the contents of their wallets. For example, a
20 man bought merchandise on a website that did not have a security padlock, and as a result of this transaction, his bank accounts were emptied. If he had paid attention to the security on the site, he would not have lost his money. However, it appears that people are becoming more aware of the risks of fraud and taking steps to avoid them since the total percentage of

incidences of fraud remained steady in 2011 (Campana, 2012). It may be that people who have
25 grown up using the Internet understand its risks as well as its strengths.

The ease of sharing information provides opportunities for crimes and abuses. While it may be impossible to entirely eliminate the risks, if people followed reasonable guidelines to protect important data, they could greatly reduce these risks. The benefits of being able to do such things as bank online, keep medical records updated almost instantly, and share the thrills both
30 big and small of everyday life with friends outweigh these concerns.

Summary–Response Essay on "Privacy and Computers"

Robert Erani, in the article "Privacy and Computers," explains the issues concerning the sharing of personal information online. According to Erani, one area of concern is that people may sometime share details of their lives online without thinking about the consequences. As the author points out,
5 "The issue now is how open one should be with sharing private information since the information could be stolen by criminals" (para. 2). The author describes a situation in which people were robbed after revealing their vacation plans online. The author further states how important it is for consumers to protect their personal information when they purchase
10 products online. Erani concludes the article by stating that, despite the concerns about privacy, one can still use online services safely by using common sense and privacy controls.

In sum, the author provides a general introduction to the issues of privacy online and offers some advice on how to avoid problems. I agree that insecure websites are
15 a problem, but I disagree with the author's contention that people who have grown up using the Internet are more savvy about using it. Hackers and scammers continue to come up with more sophisticated and convincing schemes. The consumer needs to constantly be wary of them. In addition, the article fails to address the more controversial issues concerning the consequences of posting information regarding
20 health issues, job dissatisfaction, or even political views. This is an oversight because these issues impact individuals every day. It is becoming increasingly common for employers, for instance, to view the online profiles of potential employees as part of their selection process. Despite these shortcomings, the author rightly states that the concern around privacy issues seems to be an acceptable exchange for many
25 people for the benefits of sharing their lives with others.

B *Comprehension Check* Answer these questions.

1. What two suggestions does the writer of "Privacy and Computers" make for being safe on the Internet?
2. What important issues does the summary–response writer believe are missing from the original article?
3. What other privacy concerns do you have concerning the use of your personal information? What do you do to keep your information safe?

C Notice

1 Summary–Response Writing Find the following sentences in the summary–response essay and fill in the missing words to notice how the writer refers back to the first essay.

1. _____ _____ _____ , one area of concern is that people may sometimes share details of their lives online without thinking about the consequences. (para. 1)

2. _____ _____ _____ _____ _____ , "The issue now is how open one should be with sharing private information since the information could be stolen by criminals." (para. 1)

3. _____ _____ _____ _____ how important it is for consumers to protect their personal information when they purchase products online. (para. 1)

2 Grammar Follow the instructions to notice how the author of "Privacy and Computers" uses unreal conditionals.

1. Reread the second paragraph of the article. What happened to the people who went on vacation? Underline the unreal conditional on lines 13–14. How does using an unreal conditional help the writer?

2. Reread the third paragraph of the article. What happened to the man who bought merchandise on a website that did not have a security padlock? Underline the unreal conditional on lines 21–22. How does using an unreal conditional help the writer?

3. Reread the last paragraph of the article. Find the sentence with the *if* clause. Compare this sentence with the sentence with the *if* clause in 2. Which one refers to an imagined past result? Which one refers to an imagined present result? What do you notice about the forms of the verbs?

3 The Writing Process Match the excerpts from the summary–response essay to the lines in the "Privacy and Computers" essay that it summarizes. Write the paragraph number and the line numbers in which the information appears.

1. Robert Erani, in the article "Privacy and Computers," explains the issues concerning the sharing of personal information online. Para. _____ Lines _____ to _____

2. The author describes a situation in which people were robbed after revealing their vacation plans online. Para. _____ Lines _____ to _____

3. Erani concludes the article by stating that, despite the concerns about privacy, one can still use online services safely by using common sense and privacy controls. Para. _____ Lines _____ to _____

2 | Past Unreal Conditionals

▶ Grammar Presentation

> Past unreal conditionals allow the writer to discuss hypothetical situations – untrue or unreal situations in the past – and the consequences of the situations. Effective academic writers use this form to contrast what happened (the "real") with what was possible but did not happen (the "unreal").
>
> *If the author **had discussed** education in his article, the text **would have been** stronger.*
> *If this information **had been taught** years ago, we **would not have had** so many problems.*

2.1 Past Unreal Conditionals

The past unreal conditional is formed as follows: *if* clause (past perfect) + main clause (*would / could / might* + *have* + past participle) The *if* clause can come first or last in a sentence. Use a comma when it comes first.	IF CLAUSE (PAST PERFECT) ***If** I **had read** the privacy policy on the company's website* MAIN CLAUSE (*WOULD / COULD / MIGHT* + *HAVE* + PAST PARTICIPLE) *carefully, I **would have avoided** the problem.* MAIN CLAUSE　　　　　IF CLAUSE *I **would have avoided** the problem **if** I **had read** the website's privacy policy carefully.*

2.2 Using Past Unreal Conditionals

a. The *if* clause gives the untrue condition in the past. The main clause expresses the imaginary past result.	IF CLAUSE: PAST UNREAL CONDITION ***If** she **had used** separate accounts for work and personal* MAIN CLAUSE: IMAGINARY PAST RESULT *e-mail, she **would have avoided** trouble.* (The real situation: She used the same e-mail account for personal and work e-mail. She got into trouble.) UNREAL PAST CONDITION ***If** he **hadn't made** his passwords difficult,* IMAGINARY PAST RESULT *the thieves **would have been able to access** his accounts.* (The real situation: His passwords were difficult. The thieves did not access his accounts.)

2.2 Using Past Unreal Conditionals (continued)

b. As with other forms and uses of modals, *would have* expresses a more certain (but still imaginary) past result. *Could have* and *might have* express less certain results.	*If I **had noticed** the lack of security on that website, I **wouldn't have ordered** merchandise from it.* *If I **had ordered** merchandise from that website, I **might have had** my information stolen.*
c. Use past unreal conditionals to express regrets about past situations or actions.	*If I **had insured** my laptop, the insurance company **would have reimbursed** me when it was stolen.* (I regret that I did not have insurance for my laptop.)
d. Past unreal conditionals can also express an imaginary present result. Use *would/could/might* + the base form of the verb in the main clause.	UNREAL PAST CONDITION *If the author **had mentioned** his sources,* IMAGINARY PRESENT RESULT *the article **would be more** compelling.*

▶ Grammar Application

Exercise 2.1 Past Unreal Conditionals

Read the story about identify theft. Complete the sentences with the appropriate modal and the correct form of the verb in parentheses. Sometimes more than one answer is possible.

I know that thieves have ways to steal people's identities online, so I'm always careful about the e-mails I read and the links that I click on. However, I didn't realize that thieves sometimes go through people's garbage to look for personal information. I _'d have been_ (be) more careful if I _'d known_ (know) that.

(1)   (1)

Last year, I put a letter that had my Social Security number on it in the garbage. Normally, I shred important documents, but I was in a hurry that day. If

I _____ (not be) in a hurry, I definitely _____ (shred) it.

         (2)   (2)

A few days later, there was no money in my checking account. I realized that if someone

_____ (take) the letter out of the garbage, he or she _____ (have)

        (3)   (3)

my Social Security number now. I knew that if someone _____ (find) my Social

                                             (4)

Security number, they _____ (have) the ability to access my bank accounts,

                 (4)

use my credit cards, and get new credit cards in my name.

By the time I realized that my identity had been stolen, the thief had taken all my money and applied for 10 new credit cards. If I _____ (realize) sooner that a thief had

                                       (5)

found my Social Security number, I _____ (be) able to stop him or her from

                              (5)

using it. The identity theft has caused all kinds of problems for me. I can't get a loan to buy a

car, and I can't get a new credit card. If someone _____ (not steal) my identity,

(6)

I _____ (not have) all these problems now.

(6)

     I shred all my important documents now before I throw them away. Last week, I told my

neighbor what had happened to me. She was going to put some important mail in her garbage

without shredding it. She immediately shredded the mail. If I _____ (not warn)

(7)

her, she _____ (have) the same problems that I do now.

(7)

Exercise 2.2 More Past Unreal Conditionals

A Combine the pairs of sentences describing an unfortunate event. Use past unreal
conditionals. Sometimes more than one answer is possible.

1. I visited my friend Eric for the weekend. I lost all my credit cards
   and my cell phone.

   If I hadn't visited my friend Eric for the weekend,
   I wouldn't have lost all my credit cards and my
   cell phone.

2. Eric wasn't ready to go swimming on Saturday morning.
   I went to the beach alone.

   _____

   _____

3. Eric wasn't with me. I left my wallet and phone on the beach
   while I went swimming.

   _____

4. I went swimming. Someone stole my credit cards and my phone.

   _____

5. I forgot the address of Eric's house. I couldn't find the house.

   _____

6. I didn't have my cell phone. I couldn't call Eric.

   _____

7. My cell phone wasn't password-protected. The thief was able to use my phone.

   _____

8. I had personal information on my cell phone. The thief got my bank account numbers.

   _____

9. I also forgot to wear sunscreen. I have a terrible sunburn.

   _____

B *Pair Work* With a partner, take turns describing mistakes you have made and ways that you could have avoided making the mistakes.

> *Someone stole my wallet from my purse at a restaurant last weekend. I'd hung my purse on the back of my chair. If I hadn't put it on the back of my chair, no one would have stolen my wallet. If I had put my purse closer to me, I'd have my wallet now.*

3 | Common Phrases Used in Summary–Response Writing ▶

▶ Vocabulary Presentation

> Good academic writers use phrases appropriate to introducing and identifying ideas in summary–response writing.
>
> *The article **provides** a thorough introduction to the issues of privacy.*
> *The author **fails to address** more controversial concerns.*

3.1 Common Phrases in Summary–Response Writing

a. You can use these common subject + verb combinations to introduce the main idea of a summary. They are listed in order of frequency: *The article + say, state, note, describe, mention, quote, report . . .* *The author + claim, explain, call, say, write, argue, cite, establish, start . . .* *The article* is used much more frequently than *the author* in summary–response statements. *Note:* Do not use *believe* or *think* in summary–response statements that begin with the words "*The author . . .* "	***The article describes*** *the problem of privacy and computers.* ***The article mentions*** *ways that education can prevent problems with technology.* ***The author starts the article by saying that*** *technology is part of everyone's lives.* ***The author claims*** *that the experts he interviewed for this article were well-known.* NOT *The author ~~thinks~~ that the experts he interviewed for this article were well-known.*
b. The common subject + verb combinations in (a) are usually used in the present but sometimes also appear in the simple past or present perfect. (See Unit 14 on reporting verbs.)	***The article quoted*** *many well-known sources.* ***The author has argued*** *that individuals are responsible for protecting their own privacy.*

3.1 Common Phrases in Summary–Response Writing (continued)

c. Use these phrases to identify ideas by the author of the original text:

discuss	**The article discusses** identity theft in detail.
go on to say	**The article goes on to say** that the problem is being addressed.
further state / explain	**The author further states** that regulations may be necessary in the future.
also state	**The author also states** that consumers need to become proactive on this issue.
according to the author	**According to the author**, the government has an important role in this debate.

d. Use these phrases to conclude the summary–response:

In conclusion,	**In conclusion**, the author predicts that Internet privacy will become one of the most important issues of the next decade.
In sum,	
The author concludes	
Summing up,	**Summing up**, the author calls for people to be cautious when giving their personal information online.

e. Use these phrases in the response part of summary–response writing to indicate what the author omitted or did not consider:

fail to address / mention	The author **fails to address** the idea that users are also to blame for identity theft.
not address / mention	The author **does / did not mention** that we are all responsible for protecting privacy.
Note: Phrases that use the first person, such as *In my opinion*, are rare in academic writing. They are more common in informal texts like magazines.	*I think that* the author. . .
	In my opinion, the author could have . . .

▶ Vocabulary Application

Exercise 3.1 Summarizing Information

Read the summary of an article about privacy on the Internet.
Circle the correct words or phrases to complete the summary.

John M. Eger, Chair of Communications and Public

Policy at San Diego State University, (addresses)/ claims
(1)

the issue of privacy in the Internet age in his article

"Growing Concerns Over Internet Privacy" (2010). He

starts the article / further states by explaining the historical context of the right to privacy
(2)

in the United States and **cites / describes** how in 1928, a Supreme Court decision was
(3)

made to protect the right to privacy. However, he **concludes that / notes that** our online
(4)

lives are today being monitored in ways that most people do not even realize. He then

claims / goes on to explain how websites use cookies to follow an Internet user's every move.
(5)

The author **acknowledges that / thinks that** some sharing of information may provide us with
(6)

advertisements for things that may be beneficial to us, but then he **argues that / sums up that**
(7)

data collectors might collect and share health and financial information, and even connect

our names to our data. In addition, **according to the article, / the article quotes** there
(8)

are currently no laws that adequately protect our right to privacy. Then, while the author

goes on to show / concludes by saying that we need to do something about this problem,
(9)

he **does not mention at all / further states** what we can do to protect ourselves.
(10)

Exercise 3.2 🔊 More Summarizing Information

Read the sentences below. Then listen to two people talk about an article on Internet
passwords. Make notes as you listen. Listen again and complete the sentences.

1. _The author starts the article by saying that a website_ was recently hacked.

2. _____ when they create their passwords.

3. _____ can break one password a second.

4. _____ shouldn't use the same password
   for multiple accounts.

5. _____ says, "I always use the same
   password for everything because otherwise I can't remember them."

6. _____ is abc123.

7. _____ is 123456.

8. _____ can do to create strong passwords.

4 Avoid Common Mistakes ⚠

1. Remember to use the past participle form of the verb after the modal in past unreal conditionals.

avoided
If the company had installed secure systems, it would have avoid data theft.

2. Remember to use academic, precise words rather than multi-word verbs or idioms such as:

find out	→	discover / learn
put up with	→	tolerate
start off / out	→	start / begin
look into	→	investigate

discovering
Social media users enjoy finding out what products and services their friends recommend.

tolerate
Older users will not put up with further invasions of privacy.

The article starts off with a presentation of both sides of the issue.

investigates
The author looks into recent developments in Internet security.

Editing Task

Find and correct five more mistakes in the summary paragraph from a summary–response essay on privacy issues and social networking.

In his article "Privacy and Security Issues in Social Networking" (2008), Brendan Collins
investigates
looks into the security and privacy problems associated with social networks. He starts off by making the distinction between security issues and privacy issues, pointing out that social networking sites (SNSs) provide ideal opportunities for both types of violations to take place

5 because they are so popular. As an example of a security violation, Collins cites the case of a hacker who shut down a social networking site a few years ago just for fun. It was fortunate that the attack was harmless. If the attack had been committed with a malicious intent, the personal data of millions of users would have be stolen. According to Collins, SNSs provide ideal opportunities for break-ins because they process so much information, and because so

10 many people have access to them. As an example, he describes the case of Adrienne Felt, a PhD candidate at U.C. Berkeley, who found out that there was a security flaw in a major social networking site. In other words, the same program that allowed people to share photos and send invitations also exposed their information to theft. If Felt had not looked into the

social networking site, a large proportion of users could have get their information stolen.

15 Collins goes on to recommend ways users can limit the possibility of security and privacy violations. Because SNSs are getting so big, he says, it is becoming impossible to monitor the activity that takes place on them. It is therefore the responsibility of users to take precautions as they share information about themselves. Collins concludes that there probably will never be a solution to these issues and implies that we will have to put up with threats to our privacy

20 and security. Collins adds, however, that the less one uses SNSs, the lower the chance one has of getting their identity stolen.

5 | The Writing Process ✎

In this section, you will write a two-paragraph summary–response to an article about a topic on technology. Before you start writing, you will learn about summary–response writing.

About Summary–Response Writing

Being able to create strong summary–response writing is an important skill for academic writers. Academic writers have to be able to show that they understand the ideas put forward by others and how those ideas fit into their own worldview.

The following are guidelines for writing a summary–response of an article:

1. **Identify the writer's main ideas.** While reading the original text, use a highlighter or take notes that show what the writer's main ideas are.

2. **Make notes about your own ideas.** Review your highlighted text and notes and then make more notes indicating which points you agree or disagree with.

3. **State your source at the beginning of the summary–response.** Begin your summary by giving the name of the author and the article. In your opening statement, also state as briefly as possible the writer's main point or purpose in writing the article.

   Robert Erani, in the article "Privacy and Computers," explains the issues concerning the sharing of personal information online.

4. **Refer to main ideas in the same order as in the original text.** As you summarize the article, choose the main ideas that you want to refer the reader to and identify them in the same order in which they appear in the original text. Use examples that are essential for understanding the main ideas, but only use examples from the original text – do not include your own examples.

5. **Paraphrase and use short quotations.** Use your paraphrasing skills to review the writer's ideas. Also include short quotations from the original text to give your reader a clear sense of how the writer expressed key points.

6. **In the response section, present your views clearly.** Discuss aspects you agree and disagree with. Identify ideas that the writer either missed entirely or did not develop completely. Before offering your own suggestions, it can be a good strategy to find at least one positive thing to say about the original writer's ideas. In this way, you can sound thoughtful, balanced, and reasonable.

Exercise

A Reread "Patient–Doctor Relationships in the 21st Century" in Unit 15 on pages 218–219 or "Leading a Healthy Life" in Unit 16 on pages 234–235. Then complete the following:

Summary

1. Write a sentence that identifies the source and the main point or purpose of the essay.

2. List the main ideas in the same order as in the original essay.

3. Choose one short quotation that illustrates one of the writer's key points.

Response

1. Write your overall opinion about the essay.

2. Write one point that you agree with and one point you disagree with.

3. Write one point that you believe is missing and that expresses your own idea on the topic.

B *Pair Work* Explain your ideas to a partner. Discuss any disagreements that you have. Try to convince your partner of your idea by using information from the article, your knowledge of the topic, and your experiences.

Pre-writing Tasks

Choose a Topic

A Find a short article about one of the topics listed below. You will write a two-paragraph summary–response of the article.

- Plagiarism in the digital world
- Social media and privacy
- A topic of your own approved by your teacher

B *Pair Work* Share the main ideas and details of the article you read with a partner. Express your own views on the topic of the article, noting where you agree or disagree with the writer.

Organize Your Ideas

Complete the following outline using information from the article you found.

Summary–Response Outline
Paragraph #1: Summary Source:
Main ideas:
Examples:
A short quotation:
Paragraph #2: Response Your overall view:
Ideas that you agree with:
Ideas that you disagree with:
Ideas that are missing:

Writing Task

Write your summary–response paragraphs using your outline above.
Follow the steps below.

1. In your summary paragraph, start by giving the source information, the writer's overall purpose, and main idea. Then restate the writer's main ideas in their original order without giving your own opinion.

2. In your response paragraph, find an idea or ideas of the writer's that you can agree with, and then present your own ideas on the topic.

3. Include the following in your paragraphs:
   - a quotation from the original article;
   - common summary–response phrases, such as noun / verb combinations like *the article says / states / notes* and *the author claims / explains / argues*;
   - past unreal conditionals to express what could have happened but did not;
   - at least three academic words from the essays in this unit: *area, author, aware, benefit, conclude, consequence, consumer, controversial, data, despite, eliminate, expert, financial, guideline, issue, job, media, medical, network, networking, percentage, potential, process, purchase, reveal, secure, security, selection, site, text, virtual.*

4. After you write your paragraphs, review them and make sure you avoided the mistakes in the Avoid Common Mistakes chart on page 257.

> ### Academic Writing Tip
> **In fact**
> Use the phrase *in fact* to add strong support – especially surprising information – to a preceding statement.
> *Deleting information from a computer is not always as secure as it seems.* **In fact,** *specialists can easily retrieve "deleted" files from a hard drive.*

Peer Review

A Exchange your paragraphs with a partner. Answer the following questions as you read your partner's paragraphs, and then share your responses.

1. Does the writer include the source and topic of the original article in the opening section of the summary paragraph?

2. What main points from the original article does the writer emphasize? Does the writer use the common summary–response phrases to introduce these points?

3. Does the writer avoid including his or her own opinion in the summary paragraph?

4. Does the writer include a short quotation from the original article? Underline it.

5. In the response paragraph, does the writer praise any elements from the original source material before disagreeing and offering new ideas?

6. Does the writer use any past unreal conditionals? Circle them.

7. Is anything confusing? Write a question mark (?) next to it.

8. Provide one compliment (something you found interesting or unusual).

B Use your partner's comments to help you revise your paragraphs. Use the Writer's Checklist on page A2 to review your paragraphs for organization, grammar, and vocabulary.

Persuasion 1: Nonidentifying Relative Clauses; Phrases That Limit Overgeneralization

Violence in the Media

1 | Grammar in the Real World 🌐

You will read an essay about violence on television. In the essay, the writer argues that violence on TV should be regulated by the government. The essay is an example of one type of persuasive writing.

A *Before You Read* Do you think there is too much violence shown on TV? Who do you think should be responsible for controlling the amount of violence that children watch on TV: parents, the government, or both? Read the essay. What is the writer's main argument?

TV Violence: Who Is Responsible?

Should violence on TV be regulated? This question has long been debated. Opponents defend the right to freedom of speech. Proponents believe that some restriction is essential to protect young people from too much exposure to violence. In 2007 in a controversial report, the Federal Communications Commission (FCC), which is the government agency that regulates
5 radio, TV, and Internet communications, advised the government to regulate violence on television to protect children. A report in 2010 by Brocato, Gentile, Laczniak, Maier, and Ji-Song states that children who watch violent TV shows and play violent video games are likely to exhibit more aggressive and violent behavior (para. 2). It is clear that the government should take immediate action and control violence on TV through regulations.

10   Regulation by the government should protect the public, especially children, from overexposure to violence. In the past, courts have protected violent speech and depictions[1] of violence under the First Amendment.[2] Nonetheless, the government regulates TV and film indecency.[3] According to the FCC, the Supreme Court allows these restrictions so that children are not so easily exposed to indecency. The parallel with violence in the media is obvious.
15 Limiting media violence is much like limiting indecency in the media (FCC, 2007, p. 11–12).

[1]**depiction:** an image │ [2]**First Amendment:** an amendment in the United States Constitution that allows for freedom of speech in most situations │ [3]**indecency:** behavior that upsets popular moral standards, usually as they relate to sexual behavior and nudity

Government regulation will also help parents monitor their children's exposure to violence. FCC Chairman Kevin Martin explained that while parents should always be the decision makers on how to best protect their children from violence, they alone cannot be responsible (FCC, 2007, p. 25). The main problem is that television violence seems to have a strong presence
20 in most children's lives. TV rating and program-blocking systems, which are both tools to help parents control viewing, are "not effective," according to the FCC, since networks may not consistently monitor TV shows for violent content (FCC, 2007, p. 25). In fact, the Parents Television Council, which monitors TV shows for violent content, states that networks are not doing a good job of rating TV shows. As a result, children have access to inappropriate content.

25   Congress has resisted addressing this issue. However, not addressing it could put children, who have young minds that are easily impressionable,[4] at risk. It could also put society at risk for aggressive acts committed by people influenced by violent media. Therefore, the government must act now to regulate media; otherwise, society will have a difficult road ahead trying to control the negative effects of violent media on our children.

[4]**impressionable:** readily or easily influenced

B *Comprehension Check* Answer the questions.

1. What evidence is given in the essay that violence on TV may negatively affect children's behavior?

2. Why might it be difficult in the United States for the government to regulate TV violence?

3. Do you agree with the writer that violence on TV should be regulated? Why or why not?

C *Notice*

1 Persuasive Writing Check (✓) the two arguments to regulate violence on TV that are emphasized in the essay.

Government regulation of the television industry will:

_____ generate tax revenue

_____ protect the public from overexposure to violence

_____ protect free speech

_____ reduce indecency

_____ help parents limit their children's exposure to violence

2 Grammar Answer the questions below to notice how the writer uses relative clauses to explain and support his ideas.

1. Compare the two sentences concerning children on lines 6–8 and 25–26. In which sentence does the writer refer to *all* children? In which sentence does the writer identify a particular group of children?

2. Read the two sentences on lines 20–24, starting with "TV rating and blocking systems . . ." Look at the relative clauses in these sentences. Are these relative clauses essential to understanding the sentences? What information do these clauses provide the reader?

3 The Writing Process

Pair Work Work with a partner to analyze the introduction to the persuasive essay by answering the questions below.

1. Which sentence contains the hook – a sentence that serves to create interest and motivate readers? (See Unit 2 page 30 to review the four types of hooks.) Why is this sentence an effective hook?

2. What controversial issue does the writer introduce?

3. What evidence does the writer introduce to support his or her position?

4. What is the writer's thesis?

2 | Nonidentifying Relative Clauses

▶ Grammar Presentation

Nonidentifying relative clauses provide additional information about a noun phrase. Writers often use nonidentifying relative clauses to describe or identify the proper noun or organization they are citing. The relative clause can add credibility to the expert or organization.

*The Federal Communications Commission (FCC)****, which regulates radio, TV, and Internet communications,*** *has condemned violence in children's programming.*
*Parents****, who one could argue have the most influence on young children,*** *must limit their children's exposure to violence.*

2.1 Nonidentifying Relative Clauses

a. Nonidentifying relative clauses add more details about a noun or noun phrase. They begin with a relative pronoun: *who, which, whose,* or *whom.* Use a comma before and after these clauses.	*The National Institute of Mental Health,* NONIDENTIFYING RELATIVE CLAUSE ***which is a government agency,*** *conducts research on the effects of violence on children.*
b. The information in a nonidentifying relative clause can be omitted and the sentence will still make sense.	*Brad J. Bushman and Craig A. Anderson,* ***who are on the faculty of Iowa State University****, have written extensively on violence in the media.* *Brad J. Bushman and Craig A. Anderson have written extensively on violence in the media.*

2.1 Nonidentifying Relative Clauses (continued)

c. Nonidentifying relative clauses are more common in writing than in speaking.	*L. Rowell Huesmann, PhD,* **whose research on the effects of media violence on children is well-regarded,** *argues that there is a correlation between watching violent shows and aggressive behavior.*
d. Do not use *that* or omit the relative pronoun in a nonidentifying relative clause.	*The American Academy of Pediatrics,* **which is a prominent group of medical professionals**, *has several suggestions about television violence.* NOT *The American Academy of Pediatrics,* ~~that~~ *is a prominent group of medical professionals, has several suggestions about television violence.* NOT *The American Academy of Pediatrics,* ~~is a prominent group of medical professionals~~, *has several suggestions about television violence.*
e. You can use nonidentifying relative clauses after proper nouns, such as the name of a person or an organization. This adds credibility to the source.	*Susan P. Leviton,* **who is the president of the Advocates for Children and Youth**, *is on the faculty of the University of Maryland School of Law.* *The National Violence Survey,* **which has examined violence on TV for many years**, *released its report today.*
A shorter way to indicate an expert's credentials is to use an appositive. (See Unit 12 for more information on appositives.)	*Adam D. Thierer,* **a senior fellow at the Progress & Freedom Foundation**, *believes that parents should decide whether their children play violent video games.*

▶ Grammar Application

Exercise 2.1 Nonidentifying Relative Clauses

A Underline the names of the experts in the sentences. Next, write new sentences by adding the additional information about the expert using nonidentifying relative clauses.

1. <u>Jason Edwards</u> reports that the effect of violent content on adolescents depends on how it is portrayed.

   Additional information: Jason Edwards is an assistant professor of communication at Bradford College.

   Jason Edwards, who is an assistant professor of communication at Bradford College, reports that the effect of violent content on adolescents depends on how it is portrayed.

2. A child who watches two hours of TV a day is exposed to approximately 10,000 acts of violence a year, based on research by the Philips Family Foundation.

   Additional information: The Philips Family Foundation is a nonprofit organization that focuses on health-care issues.

   _____

   _____

3. Parents should discuss the content of TV advertising with their children, according to Joanna Moore.

   Additional information: Joanna Moore is the mother of five teenagers.

   _____

   _____

4. According to Pablo Silva, the best way for children to be active is to turn off the TV set.

   Additional information: Pablo Silva studies the effects of TV on children's development.

   _____

   _____

5. In 2006, the American Academy of Child & Adolescent Psychiatry determined that children with excessive exposure to violence on television may "become 'immune' or numb to the horror of violence" (p. 1).

   Additional information: The American Academy of Child & Adolescent Psychiatry provides resources about children's mental health.

   _____

   _____

6. Gerard Jones believes that effective use of media violence can help children vent their anger.

   Additional information: Gerard Jones is a well-known comic book writer and the author of the article "Violent Media Is Good for Kids."

   _____

   _____

B *Pair Work* Find the sentences in A in which the relative clauses can be turned into appositives. Say each sentence with the appositive. Then give your opinion of the information.

Jason Edwards, an assistant professor of communication at Bradford College, reports that the effect of violent content on adolescents depends on how it is portrayed. I think I agree. When violence is portrayed as something heroic or admired, then I think it is harmful because children always want to imitate their heroes.

Exercise 2.2 More Nonidentifying Relative Clauses

A 🔊 Listen to a talk show on the effects of media violence on children. Take notes about the speakers on their credentials or information about their background and their opinion on the issue. Finally, write statements about each person. Use nonidentifying relative clauses.

1. Dr. Marc Richards

   Marc Richards, who is a school psychologist, believes that exposure to violence in the media encourages young children to react violently when they're upset.

2. Kevin McDonald

   _____

   _____

3. Dr. Marcia Chan

   _____

   _____

4. Catherine Wong

   _____

   _____

5. Dr. Eric Lopez

   _____

   _____

6. Barbara Cramer

   _____

   _____

7. Noah Friedman

   _____

   _____

B *Group Work* Take turns choosing a speaker in A, summarizing the speaker's opinion, and sharing your opinion of the speaker's ideas. Include the credentials of the speaker. After you give your opinion, ask your group members to respond with their opinions.

   A *Marc Richards, who is a school psychologist, says that exposure to violence in the media causes children to react violently when they get upset. I'm not sure I agree with him. It's true that young children are impressionable, so they may think that the violent behavior on video games, for example, is appropriate, but I think family and friends are more influential.*

   B *I think I agree with Dr. Richards more. When children see violent images over and over, I think it might make them more likely to use violence when they get angry.*

3 | Phrases That Limit Overgeneralization

▶ Vocabulary Presentation

Writers of persuasive essays need to provide facts to support their arguments and points. However, it is important to be careful about the language used to express these ideas. Some phrases can help limit overgeneralizations and make claims more accurate and therefore more credible. Limiting claims is also called "hedging."

*This statement **is likely to** cause arguments.*

*Television violence **seems to** be everywhere.*

***In most cases**, parents try to control what their children watch on television.*

3.1 Words and Phrases That Limit Overgeneralization

a. Use *seem / appear / tend / be likely* + infinitive to indicate something that is possible but not certain, or to indicate something may not be true all the time. *Seem* is the most common verb in this construction.	*Experts who study violence **seem to / appear to** disagree with one another's conclusions.* (We do not know all the experts who study violence, but from what we have read, they do not agree with one another.) *Children who watch many hours of TV every day **are likely to / tend to** be exposed to violent programs.* (We do not know that all children will be exposed to violent programs, but we suspect that it is true most of the time.)
b. Use *it* constructions like *It seems that* and *It appears that* when you believe that something is a trend, but do not have enough evidence to support it strongly.	***It seems that** parents are becoming more cautious about what programs their children should watch on TV.*
c. Use these phrases to express limits on your general claims: *in most cases, mainly, typically.*	***In most cases**, children can tell the difference between cartoon violence and real violence.* *Children will **typically** show higher levels of aggression after watching violence on TV.*
d. *According to* is the most common way to identify a specific source.	***According to** the report, the television industry is not policing itself to the satisfaction of parents.*

▶ Vocabulary Application

Exercise 3.1 Words and Phrases That Limit Overgeneralization

A Rewrite each sentence about the possible positive effects of media violence. Use the word or phrase that best fits the description of the limitation in parentheses: *according to*, *appears*, *in most cases*, *likely*, *seems*, *tend*, *typically*. Use each word or phrase once. In some cases, you may need to change some of the wording of the sentence.

1. Many parents and teachers believe children should not be exposed to any kind of violence in the media. (This is a trend, but there is not enough evidence to support this.)

   It appears that many parents and teachers believe children should not be exposed to any kind of violence in the media.

2. Children are taught to deny their feelings of violence. (This is true of some children, but not all children.)

   _____

3. Adults attempt to repress any violent reactions they have. (This seems to be true of many, but not all adults.)

   _____

4. Media violence allows people to fantasize about releasing their aggression in a safe, nonthreatening environment. (Some experts believe this claim.)

   _____

5. Violent video games provide players with an outlet for feelings of anger and frustration. (This is possible, but there isn't enough research to back this up.)

   _____

6. Constant denial of violent feelings, rather than exposure to media violence, makes people react to problems with aggression. (It is very possible, but it is not certain that this is true.)

   _____

7. Video games portray heroes as violent. (It is possible, but not true all the time.)

   _____

B *Pair Work* Work with a partner. Take turns making overgeneralizations about the topics below. Your partner will ask you to limit your generalization.

- The effects of violent video games on teenagers
- Reasons that children like to play violent video games
- The effects of violence in cartoons and movies on children

A *Violent video games always make children act violently.*

B *I think you're overgeneralizing. In some cases, some violent video games may make some children act violently, but you can't say that is true for all violent video games and all children unless you have research to back up your claims.*

4 Avoid Common Mistakes ⚠️

1. Remember to include the relative pronoun in nonidentifying relative clauses.

"Violent Video Games: Myths, Facts, and Unanswered Questions," ˄ *which was published by the American Psychological Association, establishes the connection between violence in games and violent behavior.*

2. Remember not to use *that* as a relative pronoun in nonidentifying relative clauses.

The National Institute of Mental Health, ~~that~~ *which published the article, is an excellent source of recent studies on the effects of violence in the media.*

3. Remember to use the singular form of the verb *seem* with *it*.

It ~~seem~~ *seems that not enough parents take responsibility for monitoring their children.*

Editing Task

Find and correct eight more mistakes in the body paragraph from an essay on violence in the media.

Government's Role in Violence in the Media

There is a major reason that the government should not be involved in solving the problem of violence in the media. Government control of the media is unconstitutional. It ~~seem~~ *seems* that some people feel that the Federal Communications Commission (FCC), is the government agency that regulates media such as TV and the Internet, is the best tool

5 for protecting children. However, many experts disagree. For example, the American Civil Liberties Union (ACLU), that focuses on constitutional rights, believes that government control of the media is a form of censorship. The First Amendment to the U.S. Constitution, guarantees freedom of speech, gives us the right to media that are not controlled by the government. A free and open media is the foundation of democracy in the United States.

10 However, it is important to protect children from violence. According to the ACLU, protecting children is the responsibility of parents, although it seem that many parents are unwilling to take on this responsibility. Caroline Fredrickson, is a director of the ACLU's Washington Legislative Office, points out in her article, "Why Government Should Not Police TV Violence and Indecency," was published in *The Christian Science Monitor* in 2007, that parents "already

15 have many tools to protect their children, including blocking programs and channels,

changing the channel, or simply turning off the television" (p. 2). She adds that the Parents Television Council, that is a nonprofit media monitoring organization, provides information on their website about television programs that are appropriate for children. It seem that if parents take responsibility for monitoring their children's television viewing, then we will be

20 able to have free and open media and protect children at the same time.

5 | The Writing Process

In this section, you will write an introductory paragraph and two body paragraphs of an essay about a controversial topic. Before you start writing, you will learn about introductory paragraphs to persuasive essays.

About the Introductory Paragraph to a Persuasive Essay

The introductory paragraph of a persuasive essay should arouse the reader's interest in a controversial topic, explain the nature of the controversy, and provide the writer's position.

The following three elements are required in an introductory paragraph to a persuasive essay:

1. A hook

2. A clear explanation of the controversy

3. A thesis statement containing the writer's position on the controversy

Exercise

A Read this introductory paragraph to a persuasive essay and answer the questions on a separate sheet of paper.

Video Games Are Being Unfairly Targeted

There is a war out there, but it is not in any video game. It is an attack on teenagers who enjoy playing video games that include warfare and violence. There is a growing number of adults who believe that video games are turning their children into mindless, heartless killing machines. They believe that violent video games must be censored, for the good of

5 teenage players and society as a whole. While their arguments seem valid at first glance, upon reflection, this attack on video-game violence and youth is both exaggerated and unnecessary.

1. What is the topic of the essay?

2. What is the controversy?

3. What is the hook?

4. What is the writer's position on the controversy?

B *Pair Work* Share your answers in A with a partner. Then answer the questions below together.

1. Was the hook effective? Why or why not?

2. Did the writer express the controversy clearly? Why or why not?

3. Based on the writer's thesis statement, what arguments do you think might be in the body of the essay?

4. What is your position on this controversy? Do you agree with the writer or do you have another point of view?

Pre-writing Tasks

Choose a Topic

A Choose one of the topics listed below. You will write an introductory paragraph and two body paragraphs on your topic.

• Are there any benefits to violent entertainment?

• Should children go to school year-round?

• A topic of your own approved by your teacher

B *Pair Work* Share your topic and position with a partner, and together brainstorm a list of arguments that support your position.

Organize Your Ideas

A Choose your two strongest arguments and complete the chart below.

Your thesis statement:
Argument 1:
Supporting information:
Argument 2:
Supporting information:

B *Pair Work* Share your chart with a partner. Ask your partner to "play devil's advocate," that is, to think of reasons why your arguments are weak. By thinking of weaknesses in your arguments, you will be able to strengthen them.

Writing Task

Write an introductory paragraph and two body paragraphs for your essay, using the information in your chart from above. Follow the steps below.

1. In the introductory paragraph, include a hook, a clear explanation of the controversy, and a thesis statement that expresses your point of view.

2. In the two body paragraphs, develop your arguments. Use the opinions of experts if possible.

3. Include the following in your paragraphs:

   • nonidentifying relative clauses;

   • phrases that limit overgeneralizations;

   • at least three academic words from the essay in this unit: *access, amendment, commission, committed, consistently, controversial, debate, exhibit, expose, exposure, federal, inappropriate, issue, media, monitor, negative, network, obvious, parallel, regulate, regulation, restriction.*

4. After you write your paragraphs, review them and make sure you avoided the mistakes in the Avoid Common Mistakes chart on page 270.

> ### Academic Writing Tip
>
> **Use Adverbs to Avoid Overgeneralizations**
> You can also use the following adverbs to avoid generalizing:
> *apparently, generally, occasionally, often, probably, regularly, reportedly, usually*
> *Video games **generally** portray heroes as violent.*

Peer Review

A Exchange your paragraphs with a partner. Answer the following questions as you read your partner's paragraphs, and then share your responses.

1. Does the writer's introductory paragraph contain an effective hook, a clear explanation of the controversy, and a strong thesis statement?

2. Are the arguments in the body paragraphs well supported?

3. Does the writer include nonidentifying relative clauses? If there are few or none, indicate places where the writer could add one or two.

4. Does the writer use words or phrases that limit overgeneralizations? Underline them.

5. Is anything confusing? Write a question mark (?) next to it.

6. Provide one compliment (something you found interesting or unusual).

B Use your partner's comments to help you revise your paragraphs. Use the Writer's Checklist on page A2 to review your paragraphs for organization, grammar, and vocabulary.

Persuasion 2: Noun Clauses with *Wh-* Words and *If/Whether*; Phrases for Argumentation

Living in an Age of Information Overload

1 | Grammar in the Real World

You will read an essay that discusses the easy availability of information online. The essay is an example of a type of persuasive writing in which the writer chooses to present opposing views.

A *Before You Read* How do you find most of your information: in printed sources or online sources? Read the essay. What concerns does the writer have about relying on the Internet for information?

So Much Information, So Little Time

We live in an amazing time, with access to almost unlimited information, entertainment, and opinions. Digital technology offers us new information whenever we are "plugged in." Just the other day, I watched a baseball game on TV, texted a friend, and kept track of the details of my other friends' lives online. I also kept an eye on all the other sports scores as they were
5 happening. I did all this while also having a conversation with my brother. While it is true that digital technology has many benefits, they come at a cost, producing citizens who have fewer critical-thinking skills and weaker social skills.

According to the proponents[1] of technology, easy access to information is one way that people benefit from new technology. When doing research, you do not have to walk to a library,
10 search for books, and read words on paper. Obviously, finding what we need from the Internet is faster, and online searches provide a broader range of sources. Often, however, when people are faced with search-engine results in the thousands or more, their critical-thinking skills may be overwhelmed by the sheer volume of material to read. One study in the UK showed that students skimmed over most information they found. According to this study, they rarely read
15 more than a page or two when completing academic research (Carr, 2008, para. 7).

Proponents also point out that technology has increased social connections. People can stay in touch with friends more easily now, sending them birthday greetings, sharing complaints, and keeping each other informed, all online. Naturally, e-mail and social networking websites have facilitated[2] communication. Ironically,[3] though, the tools designed for increased online
20 interaction may actually lead to people being less social. Students rarely need to engage in

[1]**proponent:** supporter | [2]**facilitate:** make easier | [3]**ironically:** in a way that is different from what was expected

face-to-face interactions these days either with their professors or their fellow students. Lonely librarians remember when students used to ask them questions in person. Now they more often respond to students' text queries via website help centers. At the end of the day, workers come home exhausted by so much online interaction. Having made themselves accessible
25 online 24 hours a day, they end up sacrificing family time at home as they prepare for the next round of virtual interaction.

Clearly, increased access to information results in added benefits, but it is also true that there is a cost. People who embrace new technology should reflect on what they lose as well as what they gain. There is a choice between touching and smelling a flower grown in my garden
30 and sharing it with one or two friends in the neighborhood, and instead photographing the flower, putting that image online, and reading the responses of my worldwide set of "friends." Perhaps the touch of the real flower should rule.

B Comprehension Check Answer the questions.

1. What are the two main points in favor of new technology mentioned by the writer?

2. Why does the writer believe that ease of access to information may not be such a good thing?

3. The writer offers readers a choice in the concluding paragraph. What point do you think the writer is making by offering a choice?

C Notice

1 Persuasive Writing

Pair Work Find examples in the essay where the writer presents views that oppose his or her own thesis, and then discuss the following question with a partner: Why do writers include opposing points of view in persuasive writing?

2 Grammar Find the answers to the following questions in the essay to notice how the writer uses grammar in her arguments:

1. Read the sentence on lines 28–29 beginning with "People who embrace . . ." to notice how the writer uses a clause with a *wh-* word to help present the different sides of the argument. What are the two sides of the argument?

2. Find the sentence in the first paragraph in which the writer states the opponent's view and then responds. What phrase does the writer use to introduce the opponent's view before refuting it?

3 The Writing Process Check (✓) which order the writer uses to organize the ideas in each of the two body paragraphs in the essay.

_____ a. Presentation of opposing viewpoint → Presentation of writer's viewpoint

_____ b. Presentation of opposing viewpoint → Refutation of (finding fault with) opposing viewpoint → Presentation of writer's viewpoint

_____ c. Presentation of writer's viewpoint → Presentation of opposing viewpoint

2 Noun Clauses with *Wh-* Words and *If/Whether*

▶ Grammar Presentation

Noun clauses with *wh-* words and *if/whether* are useful in persuasive academic writing, especially to present different viewpoints and then critique those viewpoints.

*Experts disagree on **what the benefits and drawbacks of Internet use are for students**. Nobody really knows **if children today have more difficulty with concentration**.*

2.1 Noun Clauses with *Wh-* Words

a. *Wh-* noun clauses start with a *wh-* word (*who, what, where, when, why,* and *how*) and function as nouns. They can act as subjects, objects, or objects of prepositions. In academic writing, they are more frequent as objects and objects of prepositions.	WH- NOUN CLAUSE *Readers have to decide **which** expert they trust*. *Readers are concerned about **who seems the most credible***.
Wh- noun clauses use statement word order (subj + verb). Do not put an auxiliary or modal before the subject.	*Students have to learn **how they can evaluate sources***. NOT *Students have to learn how ~~can they~~ evaluate sources*.
b. Noun clauses with *wh-* words often come after the following verbs: Thoughts and opinions: *agree, consider, disagree, know, remember* Learning and perception: *see, understand, wonder*	 *We need to consider **who our main market is***. *I don't remember **where I read that***.

2.2 Noun Clauses with *If/Whether*

a. *If/whether* noun clauses function as nouns. They start with *if* or *whether* and show an alternative choice or a *yes/no* choice. As in *wh-* clauses, these clauses are in statement word order. *Whether* is more commonly used when alternatives are presented or implied.	*Students need to check **whether their online sources are current or out-of-date***. (Alternative choice: Are they current or are they out-of-date? The answer is one or the other.) *I don't know **if that website has accurate information***. (*Yes/no* choice: Does that website have accurate information? The answer is *yes* or *no*.)
b. The verbs *know, see,* and *wonder* are commonly used with *if/whether* noun clauses.	*Let's **see** if we can find an answer on this website.* *Some students **wonder** whether they should do research online or in the library.* *I don't **know** if there are computers available to do the research online.*

▶ Grammar Application

Exercise 2.1 Noun Clauses with *Wh-* Words and *If / Whether*

Combine each pair of sentences about the effects of information overload on workers and the workplace. Use a noun clause with a *wh-* word, *if,* or *whether.* Sometimes more than one answer is possible.

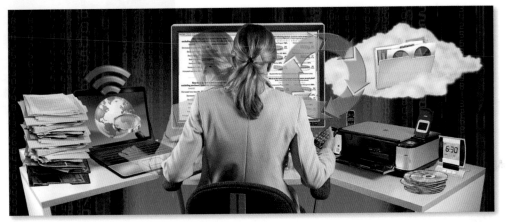

1. How does information overload affect the workplace? Researchers are studying this.
   Researchers are studying how information overload affects the workplace.

2. Does information overload make an employee more or less efficient? Researchers are trying to determine this.
   _____

3. What do employees do when they are overwhelmed by too much information? Employers want to know this.
   _____

4. Do employees ignore important facts or absorb more when they are overloaded with information? Employers wonder this.
   _____

5. Do overloaded employees waste time? Corporations want to find this out.
   _____

6. How does information overload affect employees' decision-making skills? Studies may determine this.
   _____

7. When do employees feel overwhelmed by information? Researchers wonder this.
   _____

8. Does information overload increase or decrease productivity? Researchers want to learn this.
   _____

Exercise 2.2 More Noun Clauses with *Wh-* Words and *If/Whether*

A 🔊 Listen to a lecture about information overload. Number the questions in the order that the speaker mentions them as noun clauses with *wh-* words and *if/whether*.

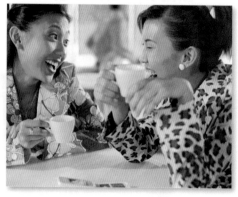

_____ 1. What is the daily volume of new web content?

_____ 2. What can we do about information overload?

_____ 3. Do you really need to send out e-mails to people who don't need them?

_____ 4. Does each recipient of information really need the information that he or she receives?

_1_ 5. How does information overload impact us?

_____ 6. Do you have to look at that video that your friend sent you?

_____ 7. What are some of the causes of information overload?

_____ 8. What can you do to avoid being overwhelmed by information?

_____ 9. Can you spend a portion of your day disconnected from technology?

B *Pair Work* Complete the summary below of the lecture in A with a partner. Use the answers in A written as noun clauses with *wh-* words and *if/whether*. Then share your paragraph with another pair.

First, the lecturer says that he wonders _how this information overload impacts us_
(1)
and _____ . Then he says he is going to examine
       (2)
_____ . Next, he tells us that people tend to distribute
       (3)
information without considering _____ . The
                                      (4)
lecturer also wonders _____ . Then he moves on to
                            (5)
consider _____ . His first suggestion is that people
              (6)
should see _____ . Second, he tells his audience
                (7)
to focus on one source of information at a time. Third, he asks people to consider

_____ . Finally, he tells people to ask themselves
       (8)

_____ .
       (9)

3 | Phrases for Argumentation

▶ Vocabulary Presentation

Writers use particular words to present an opposing view, to acknowledge that an opposing view has some merit, and to refute, or disprove, the opposing view.

It has been argued that *the Internet has caused groups to form more quickly than in the past.*

Clearly*, the Internet offers access to a wealth of information.*

However*, some students need more guidance than others in using online resources.*

3.1 Phrases That Present an Opposing View

a. Use the following phrases to present opposing documented views: *It has been argued that . . .* *It is argued that . . .* *It has been claimed that . . .* *Some researchers disagree that . . .* *Argue* and *claim* are the most common.	***It has been argued that*** *young people handle information in a much different way.* ***It has been claimed that*** *it is important for adolescents to spend time away from electronic devices.*
b. Use these phrases to present potentially opposing views when you do not have sources for your claim. Modals make the claim less strong. *It might / could / may be argued that . . .* *It might / could / may be claimed that . . .* *Might* and *could* are more common than *may*. (See Unit 16 for more practice with *it* constructions.)	***It could be argued that*** *video games allow children to develop critical-thinking skills.* ***It might be claimed that*** *cell phone use can be addictive.*

3.2 Logical Connectors That Show a Point of View

Use these adverbs as logical connectors to acknowledge a specific point of view or an opposing argument: *clearly, naturally, obviously, of course*	***Clearly****, increased access to information results in a benefit.* ***Obviously****, few want to return to the old system of information gathering.* *Internet research is different,* ***of course****, and it requires specific strategies to get proper results.*

3.3 Phrases That Introduce a Refutation

Use these phrases to introduce a refutation or to dispute an argument:

However, . . .

It is not true that . . .

That may be so, but . . .

(Unfortunately,) this is (simply) not true.

While it is true that . . .

This is (simply) not true is the most common of these phrases.

OPPOSING VIEW

Some claim that violence on TV leads to violence at

REFUTATION

*school. **However, this is simply not true**.*

OPPOSING VIEW

*While it is true that well-designed video games can help children think creatively, **they do not replace***

REFUTATION

***physical interaction with others**.*

▶ Vocabulary Application

Exercise 3.1 Phrases for Argumentation

Complete the paragraph below about some drawbacks of easy access to information. Circle the correct word or phrase.

(While it is true that)/ However, it has been argued that easy access to information
(1)
allows people to learn almost anything they want at any time, there are some downsides

to this accessibility. Some people believe that individuals are more productive when they

multitask. **Naturally / Unfortunately**, this is simply not true, according to recent studies.
(2)
Attempting to do several things at once is less efficient than doing one thing at a time. People

should attempt to focus on one source of information at a time and one piece of information

at a time. **Clearly, / It has been claimed that** people want to receive a lot of information,
(3)
though. Otherwise, they wouldn't access so many different sources of information at once.

Also, **while it is true that / it has been claimed that** social networks allow people to
(4)
stay updated on their friends' activities, they also create a big distraction. The vast amount of

information that we have to sift through cuts into time we could actually be

spending with friends. **It is not true that / Obviously**, individuals have to decide on
(5)
their own priorities, but spending time with friends face-to-face might be more valuable

than communicating with them online. A person would probably benefit greatly from

trading time spent learning unimportant information for some time spent with friends.

It could be argued that / Of course, people will not remember the 20 status updates and 5
(6)
e-mails they read after work, but they will very likely enjoy and remember a dinner

with a friend.

Exercise 3.2 More Phrases for Argumentation

On a separate piece of paper, write a short paragraph for the thesis statement in item 2. Use the example in item 1 as a model. Include the opposing view, an agreement, and a refutation. Use the phrases for argumentation to connect the ideas.

1. **Thesis Statement: The college should provide more on-campus child care for students.**

Opposing view: The college should not provide more on-campus child care.

Agreement with the opposing view: There are enough day-care facilities in the community to serve the students who need them.

Refutation: The majority of day-care centers do not have evening hours, and most students attend school at night.

Supporting information: Many students miss school because they do not have anyone to care for their children while they are at school.

Body Paragraph: *Some college personnel may argue that the college should not provide more on-campus child care. Clearly, they believe that there are enough day-care centers in the community to serve the students who need them. However, the majority of day-care centers do not have evening hours, and most students attend school at night. Therefore, many students miss school because they do not have anyone to care for their children while they are at school.*

2. **Thesis Statement: Students should turn off their electronic devices during class.**

Opposing view: Students should be allowed to have their devices on during class.

Agreement with the opposing view: Students may need to be in contact with family members or their jobs.

Refutation: Electronic devices can be a distraction in the classroom.

Supporting information: Students can become easily distracted by their devices and miss important information.

Exercise 3.3 More Phrases for Argumentation

Pair Work Work with a partner and choose a topic from the list below or a topic approved by your teacher. Choose opposing sides and, individually, write sentences to argue for your side. Use vocabulary that addresses opposing views. Then role-play a debate about the topic.

• Are parents who allow their children to spend all day using electronic devices negligent?

• Should people turn their cell phones off when they're out with friends?

• Is it acceptable to surf the Internet and check text messages during class?

A *It has been claimed that too much television is not good for young children. However, children can learn a lot from watching television. They can learn about cultures and families that are different from their own. And they can learn practical information like reading and numbers by watching educational shows.*

B *That may be so, but it is also true that children can learn even more by interacting with humans rather than with an "electronic babysitter."*

4 | Avoid Common Mistakes ⚠

1. **Remember to use *if*, and not *whether*, to express a condition.**

   if
   E-books will be popular ~~whether~~ they are less expensive than print books.

2. **Remember that *or not* can immediately follow *whether*, but it can only appear at the end of a sentence with *if*.**

   whether
   Experts can't decide if or not students retain enough information with online reading.

   or not
   Experts can't decide if ~~or not~~ students retain enough information with online reading.

3. **Remember to spell *whether* correctly.**

   whether
   The instructors decide ~~weather~~ students bring laptops or smartphones to class.

   whether
   They have not decided ~~wether~~ laptops are helpful or a distraction.

Editing Task

Find and correct six more mistakes in the body paragraph from an essay on information overload.

Information Overload

Opponents of online technology often point to the negative effects of the information
whether
age. They claim that ~~weather~~ individuals use the Internet for research or for social networking,

they suffer from information overload. They believe that easy access to information has a

negative effect on users' critical-thinking skills. They also cite the fact that online readers

5 understand and retain less than print readers. The fact is, however, that experts have not yet

determined if or not there is a difference between reading online and reading print material.

There haven't been enough studies to determine if or not there truly are negative effects of

information overload. Furthermore, it is important for proponents of this argument to identify

wether they are referring to the effects of technology on older people or younger people.

10 For example, their arguments may not be valid whether they consider how digital natives

respond to technology. Digital natives are people who were born since the 1990s. They were

born into a digital world, and they have been using technology since childhood. According

to Tapscott (2009), digital natives process information differently than digital immigrants

(people who were born before the 1990s and learned how to use the Internet later in life than

15 digital natives did). Tapscott cites a study designed to show whether digital natives retained

more information from a traditional newscast or an interactive webcast. The study showed

that digital natives remembered more from the interactive news source. Tapscott also points

out that intelligence and aptitude test scores are rising, which further indicates that digital

natives' thinking styles have not suffered. Some wonder wether digital natives should adapt

20 to traditional ways of processing information. However, if or not we like it, the information

age is here to stay. Therefore, digital immigrants are going to have to adapt to digital ways of

interacting with technology.

5 | The Writing Process

In this section, you will write two body paragraphs for a persuasive essay that will include two
opposing views and refutations of those views. Before you start writing, you will learn about
opposing views and refutations.

About Presenting and Refuting Opposing Views

In persuasive essays, writers often include views that oppose their own, and then refute
them (show why those views are not as valid or strong). In doing this, writers provide
support for their own viewpoints. The following steps can be used when writing body
paragraphs in a persuasive essay:

1. **State the opposing view.** Good persuasive writers often start to argue a position by
   recognizing that other people have points of view that should be considered. A reader
   is more likely to be persuaded by a writer who presents opposing views than by a writer
   who puts forward only his or her own viewpoint without acknowledging the existence of
   other viewpoints.

2. **Partially agree with the opposing view.** Persuasive writers can make their own case
   even stronger when they then state that the opposing view has some merit. A reader will
   believe that a writer is very reasonable if that writer is prepared to agree that his or her
   opponent has made some good points.

3. **Refute the opposing view.** Once the opposing position has been stated and shown to
   have some good qualities, the persuasive writer can now show his or her own position by
   showing the weaknesses in the opponent's viewpoints. The change in tone from one of
   reasonableness to one of refutation is usually marked by *However, . . .* or such phrases as
   While it may be true that. . . .

4. **Support the refutation.** Finally, persuasive writers need to provide evidence to support
   their own positions, not just point out the weaknesses in others' viewpoints. They do this
   by presenting supporting data and examples, citing research, and providing quotations
   from experts.

Exercise

Match the views below to the example sentences.

Views	Example Sentences
_____ 1. Presentation of opposing view	a. However, we must also consider the fact that individuals in a society have an important right to privacy.
_____ 2. Partial agreement with opposing view	b. There have been many cases over the years in which the police have been given great powers and then have used those powers in a corrupt way.
_____ 3. Refutation and presentation of own view	c. Many people argue that the police should be able to locate anyone's cell phone at any time and be given the power to listen in to cell phone conversations whenever they want.
_____ 4. Support for own view	d. It is true that this particular use of technology could indeed give the police a tremendous tool in solving crimes quickly and efficiently.

Pre-writing Tasks

Choose a Topic

A Choose one of the topics listed below. You will write two body paragraphs of a persuasive essay and argue for or against the topic. In each paragraph you will present and refute the opposing viewpoints and then argue a position.

- The use of technology in our daily lives is making our lives too complicated.
- Virtual friendships are as genuine as face-to-face friendships.
- A topic of your own approved by your teacher

B *Pair Work* Share your viewpoint on the topic with a partner. Have your partner brainstorm opposing viewpoints. Then find arguments to refute the opposing viewpoints that your partner raises. Take notes.

Organize Your Ideas

A Draw the chart below on a separate sheet of paper and complete it. Write your thesis statement, two viewpoints that oppose your thesis, your refutation of the opposing viewpoints, and support for your own position.

Thesis Statement:		
	Opposing Viewpoint 1	**Opposing Viewpoint 2**
Presentation of the opposing viewpoint		
Refutation of the opposing viewpoint		
Support for your own viewpoint		

B *Pair Work* Share your chart with a partner. See if your partner agrees that you have presented the opposing viewpoints fairly and presented the best refutations possible.

Writing Task

Write two body paragraphs that contain persuasive writing that supports the thesis statement that you wrote in the chart above. Follow the steps below.

1. Start each paragraph by presenting an opposing point of view and acknowledging one aspect of that view.

2. Continue the body paragraphs with a refutation and support for your own point of view.

3. Include the following in your essay:
   - noun clauses with *wh-* words and *if / whether*;
   - phrases to present, acknowledge, and refute an opposing view;
   - at least three academic words from this unit: *academic, access, accessible, benefit, communication, design, facilitate, image, interaction, networking, obviously, range, research, response, source, technology, text, via, virtual, volume.*

> **Academic Writing Tip**
>
> **Using Scare Quotes**
>
> Scare quotes are quotation marks used for purposes other than quoting sources. Writers use scare quotes to:
>
> 1. Alert the reader to a nontraditional or new use of a word / phrase (e.g., "plugged in" in the essay on p. 274).
> 2. Show that they disagree in some way with the meaning of a term used in a source.
> 3. Show irony or sarcasm.

4. After you write your paragraphs, review them and make sure you avoided the mistakes in the Avoid Common Mistakes chart on page 282.

Peer Review

A Exchange your paragraphs with a partner. Answer the following questions as you read your partner's paragraphs, and then share your responses.

1. Does the writer present two opposing viewpoints? What are they?

2. Does the writer agree that the opposing viewpoints have some merit?

3. Does the writer refute the opposing viewpoints and provide support for his or her own viewpoint? Mark the point in the paragraphs where this occurs.

4. Does the writer use noun clauses with *wh-* words or *if* and *whether*? Underline any you find.

5. Is anything confusing? Write a question mark (?) next to it.

6. Provide one compliment (something you found interesting or unusual).

B Use your partner's comments to help you revise your essay. Use the Writer's Checklist on page A2 to review your essay for organization, grammar, and vocabulary.

Persuasion 3: Expressing Future Actions; Common Words and Phrases in Persuasive Writing

Social Networking

1 Grammar in the Real World

You will read an essay about the impact that social networking websites may be having on college students' academic performance. In this persuasive essay, the writer argues for banning social networking sites from college campuses.

A *Before You Read* What social networking sites are popular among you and your friends? What are some possible negative aspects of social networking sites? Read the essay. Does the writer think of social networking sites as having a positive or negative impact on students? Why?

Social Networking on College Campuses

Social networking sites (SNSs) have revolutionized the way we communicate with friends, colleagues, classmates, and even family members. It is now possible to interact and maintain a relationship with someone without ever meeting in person. There are many positive aspects of these new types of interactions. However, the excessive use of such websites has created a
5 distraction[1] for some users. Some college students spend hours a day "networking" instead of focusing on their studies. To help these students be more successful, colleges and universities should block access to SNSs in most areas of their campuses.

SNSs have been growing in popularity at an astonishing rate. According to the Pew Research Center's Internet & American Life Project, it is estimated that at least 85 percent of college
10 students in the United States use some type of online social network on a daily basis (Smith, Rainie, & Zickuhr, 2011). In fact, according to many instructors, college students are growing dependent on such networks. While there is no doubt that SNSs have created valuable new ways to communicate and share information, they have also become a distraction for college students who spend time online instead of preparing for their future careers.

15 Some proponents claim that the networking phenomenon[2] can be positive. Students can join online groups in which everyone shares the same interest, and they can learn how to communicate effectively in this digital age. It has been further argued that, when online, students will discuss current events and issues that they are less likely to discuss in "real life" interactions. In an ideal world, this could indeed be a beneficial way to promote interaction with people from different cultures and backgrounds. Opponents argue that, in reality, some

[1]**distraction:** something that takes your attention away from where it should be focused | [2]**phenomenon:** something that is noticed because it is unusual or new

20 discussions provide a less rigorous platform for ideas because of the lack of monitoring and the informal nature of the format. It is therefore difficult to argue that these postings would add significantly to the students' knowledge base.

Colleges and universities should consider strong policies on the use of SNSs on campus because students waste valuable study time on them. In fact, some studies report a link
25 between time on SNSs and grades. For example, an Ohio State University survey indicates that students who regularly use SNSs study less than five hours per week and have an average GPA between 3.0 and 3.5. In contrast, students who do not use these websites study 11 hours or more per week and have an average GPA between 3.5 and 4.0 (Grabmeier, n.d.). In addition, teachers are increasingly concerned about social networking use in class. They complain that
30 students are "messaging friends or posting . . . status updates from their laptops instead of paying attention to lectures" (Hamilton, 2009, para. 7). Based on these concerns, establishing clear policies for use of these websites on campus is likely to help students focus on their studies. They would spend more time studying, and their grades should improve as a result.

Social networking sites present a new way to find, organize, and share information and
35 contacts. These visually stimulating, highly interactive websites attract many college students. However, their addictive nature can potentially disrupt[3] student life to the degree that colleges and universities have to take action and ban access to social networking sites in some areas on campuses.

[3]**disrupt:** change the normal direction and create disorder

B *Comprehension Check* Answer the questions.

1. What positive things does the writer say about social networking sites?

2. Why does the author want to limit or ban social networking sites on campuses?

3. Do you agree or disagree with the writer's point of view? Why?

C *Notice*

1 **Persuasive Writing** Match the excerpts from the essay on the left with the type of argument they represent on the right.

_____ 1. It is estimated that at least 85 percent of college students in the United States use some type of online social network on a daily basis (Smith, Rainie, & Zickuhr, 2011).	a. opinion from respected authorities or experts
_____ 2. In addition, teachers are increasingly concerned about social networking use in class. They complain that students are "messaging friends or posting . . . status updates from their laptops instead of paying attention to lectures" (Hamilton, 2009, para. 7).	b. connection between presented information and recommendations
_____ 3. Based on these concerns, establishing clear policies for use of these websites on campus is likely to help students focus on their studies. They would spend more time studying, and their grades should improve as a result.	c. facts, statistics, trends

2 Grammar Complete the tasks below to notice the grammar that the writer uses to talk about possible future events and opposing views.

1. Compare the use of the word *should* on lines 7 and 33. How are the meanings of *should* different?

2. Read the sentence on lines 31–33 beginning with "Based on these concerns . . . " Look at the verb phrase. Does the verb phrase refer to present or future time? What words in the phrase help you to determine this?

3. Look at the use of *would* on lines 21 and 33. Does the meaning of *would* refer to present time or a likely result in the future?

3 The Writing Process The writer included findings from research in the essay. Complete the table below with the authors, sources, and the information or opinion that was taken from those sources.

Name of Source	Information / Opinion Retrieved from Source
Smith, Rainie, Zickuhr	At least 85 percent of college students in the United States use online social networks daily.
Grabmeier	
Hamilton	

2 | Expressing Future Actions

▶ Grammar Presentation

To express plans, predictions, and expectations, writers use *will*, *be going to*, modals, and a variety of words and phrases.

Students **will not** be able to access social networking websites if colleges ban them.

Blocking social networking websites on campus **would** help students focus on their studies.

2.1 Using *Will, Be Going To*, and Modals to Express Certainty and Make Predictions

a. Use *will* and *be going to* to write about a plan or prediction in the future. *Will* is more common in academic writing than *be going to*.

The Internet **will continue to allow** for a greater exchange of ideas.

Some colleges **are going to ban** access to social networking sites on campuses.

2.1 Using *Will, Be Going To*, and Modals to Express Certainty and Make Predictions *(continued)*

b. Use modals *could, might,* and *may* to express possibility in the future.	The use of social networking sites by recruiters for jobs **could increase** in the next few years.
c. Use *should* to express an expectation.	New technology **should make** communication more efficient.
d. Use *would* to express an expectation based on either a stated or unstated condition.	Banning note-taking on laptops **would prevent** students from using the Internet during classes. If the school implements the ban now, it **would see** major benefits within the next few months.

2.2 Using Other Expressions to Express Future Action

a. Use these phrases to write about something that will likely happen in the near future: *is due to* *is about to*	 The new version of the phone **is due to come** out by next year. The company **is about to introduce** a new app.
b. The following phrases can be used to talk about possible future events: *it is / seems / looks likely that* + clause something / someone *is / seems / looks likely to* + verb *is / are considering* + verb + *-ing* *anticipate* + verb + *-ing* (suggests that the event is very likely)	 **It seems likely that** younger teachers will be more comfortable with educational technology. Younger teachers **are likely to be** more comfortable with using technology. The school **is considering prohibiting** all unauthorized Internet access on campus. We **anticipate focusing** only on student performance scores, not other factors.
c. The following verbs, usually in the present tense, show plans for the future: *hope to*: not definite but preferable *intend to*: not definite but preferable *plan to*: scheduled to happen	 The students **hope to maintain** their high school friendships online. The university **intends to investigate** the effects of technology on student performance. Large technology companies **plan to move** many applications to phones and other digital devices.

▶ Grammar Application

Exercise 2.1 Future Possibilities

A The managers of a design magazine have noticed an increase in the number of employees who use social networking sites at work. Read the blog post and employee comments about the issue. Circle the correct words and phrases to complete the sentences.

Friday, May 8

It has been noted that some employees are spending a lot of time on social networks during work hours, and productivity has gone down. We really need everyone to be focused right now because we **are about to** / **are considering** launch our new website,
(1)
and we **plan to get** / **anticipate getting** a lot of new business as a result. Because of this,
(2)
management **is likely to block** / **is considering blocking** social networking websites from the
(3)
office. However, we'd like to hear what you all think about this. We welcome your comments.

We **anticipate having** / **will have** a meeting next Friday at 2:00 to discuss this issue. All
(4)
employees are welcome. We **plan to** / **hope to** see all of you there.
(5)

COMMENTS:

Marta G.: Not everyone spends a lot of time on the sites. Most of us check the sites a couple of times a day. Why punish everyone? It **should be** / **seems likely** that people who waste
(6)
time **should** / **will** find other ways to waste time if they can't get on social networking sites.
(7)

Erin W.: I like this idea. It's frustrating when my team members don't complete their work because they have spent too much time online. This change **would** / **is going to** prevent
(8)
them from spending half the workday online. And my team's productivity **intends to** / **could**
(9)
increase.

Tomas K.: I use a social networking site to update my clients on the latest design trends. Some of my clients contact me during the day on this site. If I couldn't use the site at work, I
should / **might** lose some of my clients. I **intend** / **am not likely** to protest this policy if it goes
(10)   (11)
through.

Kevin L.: Friday's a bad day for this meeting. A lot of people **don't plan** / **are not likely** to
(12)
attend because they telecommute that day. You should change the day.

B *Pair Work* With a partner, create a role play between two managers of small businesses who have differing views on the use of social networking at work. Answer these questions in your role plays: What are you considering doing? How might the policies affect employees? How will employees react? How do you plan to address employees' reactions? Use modals and phrases that show certainty, prediction, and future action.

Student A You are seriously considering banning the use of social networking sites through the company's computers and implementing strict rules about not accessing them on cell phones during work hours. You strongly believe that these sites cause employees to waste time, do poor quality work, and be irresponsible.

Student B You do not believe that social networking sites should be banned at work because you believe that this will create a lot of anger and resentment from employees. You want to work with employees to create a set of policies that everyone can agree with.

A *I'm seriously considering banning the use of social networking sites at my workplace because I think they're a major distraction for my employees.*

B *I feel differently. I agree that there might be a need to have policies regarding their use, but I'm not sure that banning is the right solution. There may be other solutions. You're going to get a lot of criticism, you know.*

A *I know I am. I'm planning to hold several meetings about it....*

Exercise 2.2 ◀)) Future Possibilities

Listen to two college students, Lisa and Ben, talk about social networking sites. Write *T* if the statement has a meaning similar to the one you hear. Write *F* if the statement has a different meaning. Correct the false statements so that they are true.

_F_ 1. Their college ~~has recently blocked~~ *is considering blocking* Internet access to social networking sites in some areas on campus.

_____ 2. Ben thinks blocking access might help students study more.

_____ 3. Lisa is going to demonstrate against it if the school blocks access.

_____ 4. Ben will demonstrate against it if the school blocks access.

_____ 5. One popular social networking site is about to charge people to use their site.

_____ 6. Lisa thinks a lot of people might delete their account if the popular social networking site charges people.

_____ 7. Ben thinks that people will pay to use the popular site.

_____ 8. Lisa might use a social networking site if she has to pay.

3 Common Words and Phrases in Persuasive Writing

▶ Vocabulary Presentation

In Unit 19, you learned common vocabulary used in persuasive writing to discuss opposing views. Now you will learn how to use other common vocabulary for persuasive and other kinds of academic writing.

*According to the **proponents** of technology, easy access to information is one way that people benefit from new technology.*

*Some educators **claim** that the networking phenomenon can be positive.*

3.1 Common Vocabulary in Persuasive Writing

a. These nouns are common in persuasive writing: When referring to people, you can use: *advocates, opponents, proponents, supporters* When referring to ideas, you can use: *argument, belief, claim, conclusion, evidence, fact, information, problem(s)*	***Opponents** of social networking sites argue that these communities deter face-to-face interactions.* *The main **argument** used by **proponents** of social networking websites is that they allow contact with people from all over the world.* *Some critics see students' dependence on SNSs as a **problem**, but there is little **evidence** of this.*
b. These verbs are common in persuasive writing: *acknowledge, admit, advocate, argue, believe, claim, control, estimate, oppose, project, refute, support*	*Some people **believe** that children should not be allowed to text in class.* *A number of parents **support** banning text messaging from schools.*
c. These adjectives are common in persuasive writing: *better, illogical, important, incomplete, little, true, unproved, valid*	*It is **important** to be familiar with the latest technology.* *It is **true** that some people spend too much time in front of the computer.* *The arguments supported by these researchers are **illogical**.*
d. These expressions are common in persuasive writing: *be in favor of* (something) *be against* (something)	*Many instructors **are in favor of** receiving homework online.* *Many teachers **are against** the use of social media in schools.*

▶ Vocabulary Application

Exercise 3.1 Vocabulary in Persuasive Writing

Read the sentences about cyberbullying. Use each word once.

| argue | ~~claim~~ | in favor of | opponents | proponents |

1. Cyberbullying occurs when people, often teenagers, are teased or humiliated by others on the Internet. Many parents and psychologists _claim_ that it can cause permanent emotional damage to children and teenagers.

2. Some people _____ that cyberbullying should be categorized as a criminal offense.

3. _____ of the idea that cyberbullying be classified as a criminal offense are _____ the approach because they believe it will decrease the amount of cyberbullying among teenagers.

4. _____ of making cyberbullying a criminal offense do not believe that criminalizing cyberbullying would be effective.

| acknowledge | evidence | against | a valid point |

5. While some people _____ that cyberbullying needs to be criminalized, they worry that the law will be ineffective because it is difficult to track the perpetrators.

6. The difficulty of tracking perpetrators is _____ , but the point may not be convincing in the near future since tracking devices are rapidly improving.

7. Some people who are _____ the criminalization of cyberbullying say that creating laws making it a crime violates free speech.

8. Some researchers have found that there is _____ that educational programs in early grades are effective in reducing the incidence of bullying.

Exercise 3.2 More Vocabulary in Persuasive Writing

Pair Work Work with a partner and choose one of the topics below. Discuss different views on the topic. Use the vocabulary for persuasive writing in your discussion.

- Should children under 12 be allowed to use social networking sites?
- Should parents have access to their children's and teenagers' social networking accounts?
- Should people be "friends" with their coworkers and managers on social networking sites?

I believe that children under 12 should be allowed to use social networking sites. I acknowledge that children can get into trouble, but if they use the sites responsibly, they can learn a lot about socializing and computer skills. . . .

4 Avoid Common Mistakes ⚠

1. **Don't confuse the noun and verb form of *claim*.**

   claim
   The ~~claiming~~ that social networking is dangerous is illogical.

2. **Don't confuse the noun and verb form of *argue*.**

   argument
   The main ~~arguing~~ against using social networking sites to communicate with people is that it is superficial.

3. **Remember to use *according to*, not *according for* or *according with*.**

   to
   According ~~for~~ a recent study, young people are losing interest in social networking.

   to
   According ~~with~~ Smith, social networking is useful as an educational tool.

Editing Task

Find and correct six more mistakes in the body paragraph from an essay on social networking.

Social Networking Sites

arguments
One of the main ~~arguing~~ against social networking sites is that people sometimes reveal information on them that often should be kept private. Recently another development has provided more support for this arguing: College admissions committees are now using social networking sites as part of the application process. According for a survey by Kaplan Test

5 Prep (2010), over 80 percent of college admissions officers use social networking sites to communicate with students. The claiming that many colleges make is that they use these sites to attract new students or to stay in contact with former students. However, some colleges admit that they are also using social networking as part of the admissions process. The main arguing for using social media is that it helps colleges evaluate candidates at a time

10 when these colleges are experiencing large numbers of applicants. According with many admissions officers, colleges need all the information they can get on applicants in order to make decisions because the admissions process has become very competitive. One college interviewer in a recent survey reported that if she has to choose between two students who are equally qualified in terms of grades and test scores, she looks at their online profiles to

15 make the final decision. In addition, applicants also use social networking sites against each other. According for another admissions officer, his office often receives anonymous messages

with links to sites that have negative information on or pictures of other applicants. Many colleges and universities do not have official policies yet on whether to use social media as part of the application process. Until these policies become clearer, prospective college

20 students should keep their social networking pages private or remove anything that might make them look less attractive to admissions committees.

5 | The Writing Process

In this section, you will write a persuasive essay, which will include citations from research that you will conduct on your topic. Before you start writing, you will learn about writing strong arguments to support your point of view.

About Writing Strong Arguments

To present a strong argument, writers need to clearly identify and define their point of view and find ways to make those arguments appear convincing. The following are three methods that writers can use to make their writing more convincing:

1. **Include facts, statistics, observations, and trends based on research to support your claims.** Supporting your arguments with facts and statistical data will make your arguments stronger. Even more important is to include the sources of your information. By providing the sources, you are showing your audience that you have done your research, and you are inviting them to verify the information for themselves.

2. **Include the opinions of authorities or experts respected by your audience.** An argument will always seem stronger if you are able to provide quotations from well-known experts who hold the same position as yourself. If the experts you cite are not well known to your audience, you can convince your audience that they are authorities.

3. **Make logical connections between the information you present and any predictions or recommendations that you make.** Facts and opinions are not arguments. It is up to you to make logical connections between facts for your audience. You have to help your readers see that there may be a causal connection between facts and that therefore the course of action that you are arguing for should be taken.

Exercise

For each item, choose the type of argument strategy that is being used by the writer. Write the letter on the line.

a. Logical connection   b. Opinion of experts   c. Facts, statistics, trends

_____ 1. One study on cyberbullying has shown that the issue is widespread, with 20 percent of students reporting that they had been bullied ("Cyberbullying Research," n.d.).

_____ 2. If schools become involved, it will reduce opportunities for cyberbullying attacks.

_____ 3. According to Christina Brown and Michelle Demaray (n.d.), the authors of "School-Based Cyberbullying Interventions," school authorities must be able to identify cyberbullying, understand how it affects students, and do everything possible to create a safe learning environment.

Pre-writing Tasks

Choose a Topic

A Choose one of the topics listed below. You will write a persuasive essay in which you take a position on your topic and back it up with researched facts and opinions.

- Can educational programs prevent cyberbullying?
- Should classrooms have closed-circuit cameras to monitor teachers and students?
- A topic of your own approved by your teacher

B *Pair Work* Share your topic with a partner. Brainstorm a list of ideas to include. Suggest the sorts of facts and opinions that will be needed to support your arguments and some possible source material to go to for research.

Organize Your Ideas

A Research your topic in the library or online. Remember to find information from sources that oppose your point of view as well as those that support it. Draw the charts below on a separate sheet of paper. Write the sources and the information that you retrieved from them.

Sources	Information That Supports Your Point of View

Sources	Information That Opposes Your Point of View

B *Pair Work* Discuss the information and the logical connections you make with a partner. See if your partner finds your logic to be persuasive.

Writing Task

Write a persuasive essay. Follow the steps below.

1. Write an introductory paragraph that contains a hook, explains the issue, and provides a thesis statement.

2. Write body paragraphs that contain topic sentences that state your main ideas, present opposing viewpoints, and provide a refutation of those views.

3. Make sure your body paragraphs contain facts, statistics, and logical connections that are supported by your research.

4. Write a concluding paragraph that summarizes the main points of your essay and contains a recommendation for future action.

5. Include the following in your essay:

   • expressions that refer to future actions;

   • argumentation vocabulary;

   • at least three academic words from the essay in this unit: *access, area, aspect, beneficial, colleague, communicate, contact, contrast, create, culture, establish, estimate, focus, grade, indicate, interact, interaction, interactive, issue, lecture, link, maintain, monitor, network, networking, percent, phenomenon, policy, positive, potentially, promote, qualitatively, revolutionize, site, status, survey, visually.*

6. Create a reference list of sources at the end of your essay.

7. After you write your essay, review it and make sure you avoided the mistakes in the Avoid Common Mistakes chart on page 294.

Peer Review

A Exchange your essay with a partner. Answer the following questions as you read your partner's essay, and then share your responses.

1. Is there a thesis statement? Is the point of view clear?

2. Has the writer included any opposing views and refuted them? What are they?

3. What methods does the writer use to support his or her arguments? Does the writer use argumentation vocabulary? Underline any you find.

4. Has the writer referred to future actions or events? Circle any verbs that refer to the future.

5. Does the concluding paragraph summarize the main points and make a recommendation or prediction?

6. Does the writer include a reference list of all the sources cited in the essay?

7. Is anything confusing? Write a question mark (?) next to it.

8. Provide one compliment (something you found interesting or unusual).

B Use your partner's comments to help you revise your essay. Use the Writer's Checklist on page A2 to review your essay for organization, grammar, and vocabulary.

References

Unit 1

Grubb, A. (2011). Peak oil primer. *Energy Bulletin*. Retrieved from
http://www.energybulletin.net/primer.php

United Nations Environment Programme. (2011). *Forest facts*. Retrieved from
http://www.unep.org/wed/forestfacts/

Unit 2

Perner, L. (2008). Consumer behavior. *USC Marshall*. Retrieved from
http://www.consumerpsychologist.com/intro_Consumer_Behavior.html

United States Environmental Protection Agency. (2011, November).
Paper recycling facts and figures. Retrieved from US EPA website
http://www.epa.gov/osw/conserve/materials/paper/faqs.htm

Unit 3

Burstein, D. (2012). A minute with . . . David Jones. *Huffington Post Business*.
Retrieved from http://www.huffingtonpost.com/david-d-burstein/a-minute-withdavid
-jones_b_1288931.html

Patagonia. (2011). *Company info: Corporate responsibility*. Retrieved from
http://www.patagonia.com/us/patagonia.go?assetid=37492

Waite, L. (2007). What makes a good corporate citizen? A discussion and case study.
EzineArticles.com. Retrieved from http://ezinearticles.com/?What-Makes-a-Good
-Corporate-Citizen?-A-Discussion-and-Case-Study&id=700539

Unit 4

BP energy outlook 2030. (2011). *BP*. Retrieved from http://www.bp.com/liveassets/bp
_internet/globalbp/globalbp_uk_english/reports_and_publications/statistical_energy
_review_2011/STAGING/local_assets/pdf/2030_energy_outlook_booklet.pdf

Brown, L. R. (2009). *Plan B 4.0: Mobilizing to save civilization*. New York, NY: W. W. Norton &
Company.

Energy today and tomorrow. (2008). *ACCENT*. Retrieved from
http://www.atmosphere.mpg.de/enid/Nr2JuneO5_Context_4pu.html

Evans, S. (2007). The benefits of wind power. *Green Living Ideas*. Retrieved from
http://www.greenlivingideas.com/topics/alternative-energy/wind-energy/the-benefits-of
-wind-power

Our dependence on oil. (2010). *Environmental Defense Fund*. Retrieved from
http://apps.edf.org/page.cfm?tagID=58983

Sweet, P. (2007). Insiders see solar energy industry as ready for takeoff. *Las Vegas Sun*. Retrieved from http://www.lasvegassun.com/news/2007/aug/19/insiders-see-solar -energy-industry-as-ready-for-ta/

The true costs of petroleum: The community map. (2003). *Ecology Center*. Retrieved from http://ecologycenter.org/erc/petroleum/community.html

Unit 5

Kochan, M. (2006). Birth order and adult sibling relationships. *Revolution Health Group*. Retrieved from www.revolutionhealth.com/healthy-living/relationships/friends-family/ parents-siblings/birth-order

Petersen, A. (2010). A dose of sibling rivalry. *The Wall Street Journal*. Retrieved from http://online.wsj.com/article/SB10001424052748704388504575419444247971432.html

Unit 6

Bureau of Labor Statistics. (2011, June). *American time use survey summary*. Retrieved from BLS website http://www.bls.gov/news.release/atus.nr0.htm

Robinson, L. N. (2011). Gender inequality. *InsideCounsel*, 22(238), 12. Retrieved from http://www.ccwomenofcolor.org/press/Gender_Inequality_10-11.pdf

Sasso, A. T., Richards, M. R., Chou, C., & Gerber, S. E. (2011). The $16,819 pay gap for newly trained physicians: The unexplained trend of men earning more than women. *Health Affairs*. Retrieved from http://content.healthaffairs.org/content/30/2/193.short

Unit 7

Clutter, A., & Nieto, R. (n.d.). *Understanding the Hispanic culture*. Retrieved from Ohio State University website http://ohioline.osu.edu/hyg-fact/5000/5237.html

Dr. Spock: Cultural differences in parenting. (n.d.). *Parents: Healthy Kids, Happy Families*. Retrieved from http://www.parents.com/parenting/better-parenting/teaching -tolerance/cultural-differences-parenting/

Unit 8

Galanti, G. (2000). An introduction to cultural differences. *The Western Journal of Medicine, 172*(5), 335–336.

Unit 9

Davis, S., Jenkins, G., & Hunt, R. (2003). *The pact: Three young men make a promise and fulfill a dream*. New York, NY: Riverhead Books.

Rodriguez, G. (2010). The American dream: Is it slipping away? *Los Angeles Times*. Retrieved from http://articles.latimes.com/2010/sep/27/opinion/la-oe-rodriguez-dream-20100927

Unit 10

Diner, H. (2008). Immigration and U.S. history. *America.gov*. Retrieved from http://www.america.gov/st/peopleplace-english/2008/February/20080307112004ebyessedo0.1716272.html

Economic impact of immigration in the twentieth century. (2011). *DISCovering Collection*. Gale. Retrieved from Portland Community College website https://library.pcc.edu

Migration – types of migration, theories on migration, migration and the family, migration and the global economy. (n.d.). The Marriage and Family Encyclopedia. JRank. Retrieved from http://family.jrank.org/pages/1173/Migration.html

Unit 12

Great Performances online: Howard Gardner's Multiple Intelligences. (n.d.) Used by permission of *WNET New York Public Media*. Retrieved from PBS online http://www.pbs.org/wnet/gperf/education/ed_mi_overview.html

Holland, J. L. (1997). *Making vocational choices: A theory of vocational personalities and work environments* (3rd ed.). Odessa, FL: Psychological Assessment Resources.

Unit 13

Barnard, N. D. (2011). Weird science: Should you say no to GM foods? *Vegetarian Times*, (384) 26.

Byrne, P. (2010). *Labeling of genetically engineered foods*. Retrieved from Colorado State University Extension website http://www.ext.colostate.edu/pubs/foodnut/09371.html

The Center for Food Safety. (n.d.). *Genetically engineered crops*. Retrieved from The Center for Food Safety website http://www.centerforfoodsafety.org/campaign/genetically-engineered-food/crops/

DeNoon, D. J. (2010). Genetically engineered salmon: FAQ. *MedicineNet*. Retrieved from http://www.medicinenet.com/script/main/art.asp?articlekey=120016

GM crops: Costs and benefits. (n.d.). Retrieved from University of Michigan website http://sitemaker.umich.edu/sec006group5/gm_food

Harder, B. (2008). Thinking Harder: Will we all soon eat lab-grown meat? *U.S. News & World Report*. Retrieved from http://www.usnews.com/science/blogs/thinking-harder/2008/04/24/will-we-all-soon-eat-lab-grown-meat

Katel, P. (2010). Food safety. *CQ Researcher* (20), 1037–1060. Retrieved from http://0-library.cqpress.com.library.pcc.edu/cqresearcher/

Kintisch, E. (2001). Why label food? Sticker shock. *The New Republic*. Retrieved from The Alliance for Better Foods website http://www.betterfoods.org/News/Archives/01_22_01.htm

Trivieri, L. (2011). The truth behind the definition of organic foods and farming. *Integrative Health Review*. Retrieved from http://www.integrativehealthreview.com/eating-nutrition/the-benefits-of-organic-foods/

Unit 14

American Academy of Child & Adolescent Psychiatry. (2011). *Obesity in children and teens.* Retrieved from http://www.aacap.org/cs/root/facts_for_families/obesity_in_children _and_teens

Bellows, L., & Roach, J. (2011). *Childhood overweight.* Retrieved from Colorado State University Extension website http://www.ext.colostate.edu/pubs/foodnut/09317.html

Bill Clinton on childhood obesity. (2010). *The Daily Beast.* Retrieved from http://www.thedailybeast.com/newsweek/videos/2010/03/17/bill-clinton-on-childhood -obesity.html

Carey, B. (2011). Parents urged again to limit TV for youngest. *The New York Times.* Retrieved from http://www.nytimes.com/2011/10/19/health/19babies.html?_r=1

Centers for Disease Control and Prevention. (2011, October). *Tips for parents – Ideas to help children maintain a healthy weight.* Retrieved from http://www.cdc.gov/healthyweight/children/index.html

A Change of Pace Foundation. (n.d.). *Childhood obesity.* Retrieved from http://www.changeofpace.org/childhoodobesity.html

Dietary guidelines for Americans, 2005. (2005). Retrieved from U.S. Department of Health and Human Services and U.S. Department of Agriculture website http://www.health.gov/dietaryguidelines/dga2005/document/html/executivesummary.htm

Puhl, R. (2011). Childhood obesity and stigma. *Obesity Action Coalition.* Retrieved from http://www.obesityaction.org/magazine/oacnews7/childhoodobesity.php

Virginia Foundation for Healthy Youth. (2010, April). *Virginia childhood obesity survey.* Retrieved from http://www.healthyyouthva.org/survey.asp

Unit 15

Fox, S. (2011). Health topics. *Pew Research Center's Internet & American Life Project.* Retrieved from http://pewinternet.org/reports/2011/HealthTopics.aspx

Torrey, T. (2009). Are you a cyberchondriac? Do you self-diagnose yourself using the Internet? *About.com.* Retrieved from http://patients.about.com/od/researchandresources/a/ cyberselfdiag.htm

Unit 16

Wong, J. (2010). 'Lack of time' biggest excuse for unhealthy eating. *AFN Thought for Food.* Retrieved from http://www.ausfoodnews.com.au/2010/03/04/lack-of-time-biggest -excuse-for-unhealthy-eating.html

Unit 17

Campana, J. (2012). Identity theft and fraud complaints up 19% in 2011. *Examiner.com.* Retrieved from http://www.examiner.com/identity-theft-in-national/identity-theft-and -fraud-complaints-up-19-2011-review

Collins, B. (2008). Privacy and security issues in social networking. *Fast Company.* Retrieved from http://www.fastcompany.com/articles/2008/10/social-networking-security.html

Eger, J. M. (2010). Growing concerns over Internet privacy. *San Diego State University News Center.* Retrieved from http://newscenter.sdsu.edu/sdsu_newscenter/news.aspx?s=72621

Unit 18

American Academy of Child & Adolescent Psychiatry. (2006). *Children and video games: Playing with violence*. Retrieved from http://www.aacap.org/cs/root/facts_for_families/children_and_video_games_playing_with_violence

Brocato, E. D., Gentile, D. A., Laczniak, R. N., Maier, J. A., & Ji-Song, M. (2010). Television commercial violence: Potential effects on children. *The Journal of Advertising*. Retrieved from Access My Library website http://www.accessmylibrary.com/article-1G1-248188461/television-commercial-violence-potential.html

Federal Communications Commission. (2007). *In the matter of violent television programming and its impact on children* (MB Docket No. 04-261). Washington, DC: Author.

Fredrickson, C. (2007). Why government should not police TV violence and indecency. *Buffalo News*. Retrieved from The Christian Science Monitor website http://www.csmonitor.com/2007/0906/p09s01-coop.html

Unit 19

Carr, N. (2008). Is Google making us stupid? *The Atlantic*. Retrieved from http://www.theatlantic.com/magazine/archive/2008/07/is-google-making-us-stupid/6868/

Tapscott, D. (2009). *Grown up digital: How the net generation is changing your world* (pp. 97–112). New York, NY: McGraw-Hill.

Unit 20

Brown, C. F., & Demaray, M. K. (n.d.). School-based cyberbullying interventions. *Education.com*. Retrieved from http://www.education.com/reference/article/school-based-cyberbullying-interventions/?page=3

Cyberbullying research. (n.d.). *Cyberbullying Research Center*. Retrieved from http://www.cyberbullying.us/research.php

Grabmeier, J. (n.d.). Study finds link between Facebook use, lower grades in college. *Ohio State University*. Retrieved from http://researchnews.osu.edu/archive/facebookusers.htm

Hamilton, A. (2009). What Facebook users share: Lower grades. *Time*. Retrieved from http://www.time.com/time/business/article/0,8599,1891111,00.html

Kaplan test prep's 2010 survey of college admissions officers. (2010). *Kaplan Test Prep*. Retrieved from http://press.kaptest.com/research-and-surveys/kaplan-test-preps-2010-survey-of-college-admissions-officers

Smith, A., Rainie, L., & Zickuhr, K. (2011). College students and technology. *Pew Research Center's Internet & American Life Project*. Retrieved from http://pewinternet.org/reports/2011/college-students-and-technology

Sources

The following sources were consulted during the development of *Grammar and Beyond Student's Book 4.*

Unit 1

Animals: Nat Geo wild: Bald eagle. (n.d.). *National Geographic.* Retrieved from http://animals.nationalgeographic.com/animals/birds/bald-eagle/

Blue Planet Network. (2010). *The facts about the global drinking water crisis.* Retrieved from http://blueplanetnetwork.org/water/facts

Department of Energy and Environmental Protection. (2010, October). *Bald eagle.* Retrieved from DEEP website http://www.ct.gov/dep/cwp/view.asp?q=325972

Hopkins, S. (2010). Geothermal energy in Iceland. *Green Chip Stocks.* Retrieved from http://www.greenchipstocks.com/articles/geothermal-energy-in-iceland/740

The Ministry for the Environment. (2002). *Welfare for the future: Iceland's national strategy for sustainable development 2002–2020.* Retrieved from http://eng.umhverfisraduneyti.is/media/PDF_skrar/Sjalfbar__roun_enska.pdf

Rosenthal, D. (2011). Iceland has the world's cleanest electricity. *Time.* Retrieved from http://www.time.com/time/magazine/article/0,9171,2042236,00.html

Sahagun, L. (2011). Wind power turbines in Altamont Pass threaten protected birds. *Los Angeles Times.* Retrieved from http://articles.latimes.com/2011/jun/06/local/la-me-adv-wind-eagles-20110606

Unit 2

Aitchison, S. (2012). Advertising Authority. *Klipsun magazine.* Retrieved from http://www.klipsunmagazine.com/?p=3779

Department of Energy & Environmental Protection. (2011). *Fun tidbits about recycling, energy and climate change.* Retrieved from http://www.ct.gov/dep/cwp/view.asp?a=2714&q=440320&depNav_GID=1645

Green living: Recycle glass. (n.d.). *National Geographic.* Retrieved from http://greenliving.nationalgeographic.com/recycle-glass/

Lavack, A. M. (2002). Advertising of unhealthy products. *Gale Encyclopedia of Public Health.* Retrieved from http://www.ask.com/health/galecontent/advertising-of-unhealthy-products

Neer, K. (n.d.). How product placement works. *HowStuffWorks.* http://money.howstuffworks.com/product-placement3.htm

Sauer, A. (2011). Announcing the Brandcameo Product Placement Award winners. *Brandchannel.* Retrieved from http://www.brandchannel.com/home/post/2011/02/22/2010-Brandcameo-Product-Placement-Awards.aspx

Story, M., & French, S. (2004). Food advertising and marketing directed at children and adolescents in the US. *International Journal of Behavioral Nutrition and Physical Activity.* Retrieved from http://www.ijbnpa.org/content/1/1/3

Unit 3

Ferrell, O. C., Fraedrich, J., & Ferrell, L. (2002). *Business ethics: Ethical decision making and cases*. Boston: Houghton Mifflin Company.

Unit 4

Cru, M. (2010). Paris metro body heat to warm up building. *Reuters*. Retrieved from http://www.reuters.com/article/2010/09/06/us-heat-metro-paris-idUSTRE68522420100906

Denmark. (2010). *ThinkGlobalGreen.org*. Retrieved from http://thinkglobalgreen.org/denmark.html

Facts about wind power. (2010). *VERA*. Retrieved from http://www.northeastwind.com/resources/facts-about-wind-power

Harrell, E. (2010). The 50 best inventions of 2010. *Time*. Retrieved from http://www.time.com/time/specials/packages/article/0,28804,2029497_2030623_2029815,00.html

Lazari, S. (2006). Energy tax policy: History and current issues. *CRS report for Congress*. Retrieved from http://fpc.state.gov/documents/organization/70315.pdf

Ozcanli, O. C. (2010). Turning body heat into electricity. *Forbes*. Retrieved from http://www.forbes.com/2010/06/07/nanotech-body-heat-technology-breakthroughs-devices.html

Paulsen, M. (2011). Wind power prices drop to coal power levels: Bloomberg. *The Hook*. Retrieved from http://thetyee.ca/Blogs/TheHook/Environment/2011/02/14/Wind-power-prices-drop-to-coal-power-levels/

Piccinotti, A. (n.d.). The oil fuel issue. *Regia Marina Italiana*. Retrieved from http://www.regiamarina.net/detail_text.asp?nid=125&lid=1

Sekiguchi, T., & Roosevelt, M. (2002). The winds of change. *Time*. Retrieved from http://www.time.com/time/magazine/article/0,9171,1003118,00.html

Unit 5

DiProperzio. (2010). Understanding the power of birth order. *TODAY Parenting*. Retrieved from http://today.msnbc.msn.com/id/39459807/ns/today-parenting_and_family/t/understanding-power-birth-order/

Rawlings, S. W. (n.d.). Population profile of the United States. *United States Census Bureau*. Retrieved from http://www.census.gov/population/www/pop-profile/hhfam.html

Rosenberg, M. (2011). China's one child policy. *About.com*. Retrieved from http://geography.about.com/od/populationgeography/a/onechild.htm

Serena Williams vs Venus Williams. (n.d.). *Diffen.com*. Retrieved from http://www.diffen.com/difference/Serena_Williams_vs_Venus_Williams

Women's grand slam title winners. (2012). *ESPN.com*. Retrieved from http://espn.go.com/sports/tennis/history/_/type/women

Yarrow, A. L. (2009). History of U.S. children's policy, 1900–present. *First focus: Making children and families the priority*. Retrieved from http://www.pcya.org/SiteCollectionDocuments/History%20of%20US%20Children%27s%20Policy%20%28Yarrow%29.pdf

Unit 6

10 key areas of Title IX: Athletics. (n.d.). *TitleIX.info*. Retrieved from http://www.titleix.info/10 -Key-Areas-of-Title-IX/Athletics.aspx

Chen, P. (2010). Do women make better doctors? *The New York Times*. Retrieved from http://www.nytimes.com/2010/05/06/health/06chen.html

Francis, D. R. (n.d.). Why do women outnumber men in college? *The National Bureau of Economic Research*. Retrieved from http://www.nber.org/digest/jan07/w12139.html

Garber, G. (2001). Landmark law faces new challenges even now. *ESPN.com*. Retrieved from http://espn.go.com/gen/womenandsports/020619title9.html

Goldin, C. (2006). Women's educational attainment and early choices. *Harvard University Department of Economics*. Retrieved from http://www.economics.harvard.edu/faculty/ goldin/files/QuietRevolution.pdf

Goudreau, J. (2010). Most popular college majors for women. *Forbes*. Retrieved from http://www.forbes.com/2010/08/10/most-popular-college-degrees-for-women-forbes -woman-leadership-education-business.html

Jones, A. (2012). Five male centered professions that women are moving into. *Elephant*. Retrieved from http://www.elephantjournal.com/2012/03/five-male-centered-professions -that-women-are-moving-into--anthony-jones/

Leaving men behind: Women go to college in ever-greater numbers. (2007). *Education-Portal.com*. Retrieved from http://education-portal.com/articles/ Leaving_Men_Behind_Women_Go_to_College_in_Ever-Greater_Numbers.html

Ludden, J. (2011). Ask for a raise? Most women hesitate. Retrieved from http://www.npr.org/2011/02/14/133599768/ask-for-a-raise-most-women-hesitate

Mather, M., & Adams, D. (2007). The crossover in female-male college enrollment rates. *Population Reference Bureau*. Retrieved from http://www.prb.org/Articles/2007/CrossoverinFemaleMaleCollegeEnrollmentRates.aspx

Needleman, S. E. (2010). Is workplace advancement gender neutral? *WSJ Blogs: The Juggle*. Retrieved from http://blogs.wsj.com/juggle/2010/02/01/is-workplace-advancement -gender-neutral-men-and-women-disagree/

Professional women: Vital statistics. (2010). *DPE Research Department*. Retrieved from http://www.pay-equity.org/PDFs/ProfWomen.pdf

Williams, A. (2010). The new math on campus. *The New York Times*. Retrieved from http://www.nytimes.com/2010/02/07/fashion/07campus.html?pagewanted=all

Unit 7

Advertising quotes. (n.d.). *Altius Directory*. Retrieved from http://www.altiusdirectory.com/Business/advertising-quotes.php

International community resources: Cultural differences. (n.d.). Retrieved from Iowa State University Center for Excellence in Learning and Teaching website http://www.celt.iastate.edu/international/CulturalDifferences3.html

Unit 8

Counting the hours. (2008). *OECD Observer*. Retrieved from
    http://www.oecdobserver.org/news/fullstory.php/aid/2480/Counting_the_hours.html

Cross cultural differences that affect web design. (2010). *Cenango*. Retrieved from
    http://www.cenango.com/blog/2010/08/cross-cultural-differences-that-affect-web-design/

Kwintessential. (n.d.). *International etiquette guide*. Retrieved from
    www.kwintessential.co.uk/resources/country-profiles.html

Würtz, E. (2005). A cross-cultural analysis of websites from high-context cultures and
    low-context cultures. *Journal of Computer-Mediated Communication*, 11(1), article 13.
    Retrieved from http://jcmc.indiana.edu/vol11/issue1/wuertz.html

Unit 11

Types of colleges: The basics. (n.d.). *The College Board*. Retrieved from
    https://bigfuture.collegeboard.org/find-colleges/college-101/types-of-colleges-the-basics

Types of interviews. (n.d.). *About.com: Job searching*. Retrieved from
    http://jobsearch.about.com/od/interviewsnetworking/a/interviewtypes.htm

Unit 12

Careers for ISTJ personality types. (2011). *BSM Consulting, Inc*. Retrieved from
    http://www.personalitypage.com/html/ISTJ_car.html

Holland personality types. (2008). *North Carolina Career Resource Network*. Retrieved from
    http://www.soicc.state.nc.us/soicc/planning/jh-types.htm

Jones, L. K. (n.d.). Holland's theory of career choice and you. *The Career Key*. Retrieved from
    http://www.careerkey.org/asp/your_personality/hollands_theory_of_career_choice.html

United States Courts. (n.d.). *Glossary of legal terms*. Retrieved from
    http://www.uscourts.gov/common/glossary.aspx

Unit 13

GMOs gain ground for the tenth consecutive year. (2006). *GMO Compass*. Retrieved from
    http://www.gmo-compass.org/eng/agri_biotechnology/gmo_planting/194.docu.html

Madrigal, A. (2008). Scientists flesh out plans to grow (and sell) test-tube meat. *Wired.com*.
    Retrieved from http://www.wired.com/science/discoveries/news/2008/04/invitro_meat

Schneider, A. (2009). Scientists create lab-grown pork. *The KT Radio Network*. Retrieved from
    http://www.ktradionetwork.com/health/scientists-create-lab-grown-pork/

Smith, P. (2011). The environmental benefits of test-tube meat. *GOOD Worldwide, LLC*.
    Retrieved from http://www.good.is/post/the-environmental-benefits-of-test-tube-meat/

Unit 14

Centers for Disease Control and Prevention. (2010, January). *Obesity & genetics*. Retrieved
    from http://www.cdc.gov/Features/Obesity/

Centers for Disease Control and Prevention. (2011, January). *Genomics and health*.
    Retrieved from http://www.cdc.gov/genomics/resources/diseases/obesity/obesedit.htm

Unit 16

U.S. Department of Health & Human Services. (2011). *Get enough sleep*. Retrieved from healthfinder.gov http://healthfinder.gov/prevention/ViewTopicFull.aspx?topicID=68

Unit 18

Anderson, C. A. (2003). Violent video games: Myths, facts, and unanswered questions. *American Psychological Association*. Retrieved from http://www.apa.org/science/about/psa/2003/10/anderson.aspx

Beresin, E. V. (2011). The impact of media violence on children and adolescents: Opportunities for clinical interventions. *American Academy of Child and Adolescent Psychiatry*. Retrieved from http://www.aacap.org/cs/root/developmentor/the_impact_of_media_violence_on_children_and_adolescents_opportunities_for_clinical_interventions

Unit 20

Cohen, J. (2011). Report: Facebook profiles are now part of 80% colleges' admissions outreach. *All Facebook*. Retrieved from http://www.allfacebook.com/report-facebook-profiles-are-now-part-of-80-colleges-admissions-decisions-2011-02

Driscoll, E. (2011). Attention college applicants: Admissions can see your Facebook page. *Fox Business*. Retrieved from http://www.foxbusiness.com/personal-finance/2011/03/23/attention-college-applicants-admissions-facebook-page/

Hechinger, J. (2008). College applicants, beware: Your Facebook page is showing. *The Wall Street Journal*. Retrieved from http://online.wsj.com/article/SB122170459104151023.html

Appendices

1. Parts of an Essay

INTRODUCTORY PARAGRAPH

Elements of Academic Writing

Writing in an academic style is necessary to succeed in school and in many jobs. **Nevertheless, this type of writing can seem overwhelming to students, who are used to a more informal style of writing, such as texting.** Understanding the key elements of academic writing can make it easier to manage. **Effective academic writing requires strong academic vocabulary, reliable sources, and clear organization.**

Hook – draws reader in

Thesis Statement – gives main idea

BODY PARAGRAPH 1

Using the right vocabulary is essential. Writers should use precise and formal vocabulary to explain their ideas. For example, in conversation someone might say, "Sometimes kids have too much stuff to do, and they can't study." In academic writing, this might be expressed as, "Sometimes students have too many commitments, so it can be difficult for them to study." One resource that can help students build their academic vocabulary is the Academic Word List **(Coxhead, 2000)**, which identifies vocabulary that is commonly found in all disciplines. Some of these words include *achieve*, *potential*, and *similar*.

Topic Sentence

Supporting Details

Citation – shows the source of the information

BODY PARAGRAPH 2

Another important skill is researching and citing sources. Academic writers should use reliable sources in their research and avoid sources that are biased. Writers must also avoid plagiarism by including the sources of all outside information. In academic writing, not providing a source of information is like cheating and can lead to serious consequences.

Topic Sentence

Supporting Details

BODY PARAGRAPH 3

It is also necessary to organize ideas appropriately. Typically, essays contain an introductory paragraph, body paragraphs with supporting details, and a concluding paragraph that summarizes or restates the main points. In addition, different writing assignments, such as research reports and persuasive arguments, can have different patterns of organization. Good writers choose patterns that are appropriate for their purpose in writing.

Topic Sentence

Supporting Details

CONCLUDING PARAGRAPH

In sum, academic essays have precise and formal vocabulary, information that is cited, and a clear organizational pattern. When writers understand the elements of academic writing, they become more effective writers. Mastering this skill can benefit students in college and, later, professionally.

REFERENCES

References

Coxhead, A. (2000). "A new academic word list." *TESOL Quarterly* **34**(2): 213–238.

2. Writer's Checklist

		Yes	No
Audience	1. Is it clear who my audience is?		
	2. Is there anything I could do to make it clearer who my audience is?		
Purpose	1. Does my writing show that I understood the writing assignment?		
	2. Is the genre (cause and effect, problem–solution) clear?		
Length	Have I stayed within the minimum/maximum length?		
Organization	1. Did I follow my outline or other organizational structure I created for the writing assignment?		
	2. For paragraph writing assignments:		
	a. Does each paragraph have a topic sentence and address one main idea?		
	b. Do I support my topic sentence with clear examples, facts, and explanations?		
	3. For essay writing assignments:		
	a. Does the introductory paragraph introduce the topic?		
	b. Is there a hook that works well?		
	c. Do I have a clear thesis statement?		
	d. Does the essay address the topic and the thesis statement?		
	e. Do I have an effective conclusion?		
	4. Have I effectively used the writing point from this unit?		
Grammar	1. Do all my sentences have subjects and verbs?		
	2. Do all the subjects and verbs agree in number?		
	3. Are the forms of verbs correct?		
Vocabulary	1. Have I used the correct forms of words (e.g., the noun form or the adjective form)?		
	2. Have I avoided informal vocabulary or slang?		
	3. Are my vocabulary choices specific and clear?		
	4. Have I used connectors, such as demonstratives (*this, that*, etc.), transition words and phrases (*Therefore, However, In addition*, etc.), and pronouns (*it, they*, etc.), to connect ideas?		
Sources	1. Have I cited information that is from outside sources?		
	2. Is it clear to my reader what the source for each idea is?		
Your Questions	1.		
	2.		

3. About Plagiarism
Definition of Plagiarism

Plagiarism is considered a form of stealing in which a writer uses another writer's ideas and/or words improperly. As a writer, you plagiarize when you:

1. copy exact words from a source without noting the name of the source and using quotation marks.
2. paraphrase in a way that is too similar to the writer's original wording, i.e., when you replace only a few words in a sentence with synonyms.
3. state specific information, for example, unique ideas, results of a study or statistics, without identifying its source.

Reasons to Avoid Plagiarism

Plagiarism is a serious offense because it is considered to be both dishonest and unethical. Educational institutions have strict policies concerning plagiarism. Students who plagiarize could risk a failing grade or even being expelled. Therefore, it is essential for you to find out all you can about your school's policies on plagiarism and learn strategies to avoid plagiarizing.

There are other important reasons to avoid plagiarism. Writers typically feel a sense of ownership about their writing, especially when they have spent a lot of time and effort to do research and to create original and effective material. Citing a writer's ideas and original text is a way to respect the person's contributions. While many people talk about plagiarism as an issue of ownership, in the end, it may be more useful to think of it as "intellectual honesty."

Another reason involves your effectiveness as a writer. Taking language without paraphrasing it or ideas without citing them may create a false sense of your understanding of the information. In other words, when you cut and paste information from someone's work into your essay, you may not really understand the information, and you may use it improperly. Also, if questioned about the material, you may not be able to respond effectively.

Finally, when a writer uses language or ideas from another source without identifying that source, it makes it difficult for the reader to find out more information about what you have written and about the topic. The citations connect readers to credible sources of information.

How to Avoid Plagiarism

Whenever you use a writer's original words or ideas in your essay, you must credit the source in the text and in a reference list that follows your essay. In order to avoid plagiarism:

1. Use quotation marks around exact words from a source and cite the source in the text using APA or MLA style. This book uses APA style in citing in-text sources, e.g., (Brooks, 2010, p. 3).
2. Paraphrase (restate in your own words) the sentences that you want to include and cite the source in the text. See Unit 4 p. 60 for a list of paraphrasing strategies.
3. Cite the source of a unique idea or specific information, such as a statistic.
4. Include a reference list at the end of your essay that has an entry for each citation in your essay.

How to Identify Plagiarism

Original Source	Excerpts From Students' Writing	Is This Plagiarism?
Primary and secondary characteristics of culture (Purnell & Paulanka, 2005, pp. 2–3) Major influences that shape people's worldview and the extent to which people identify with their cultural group of origin are called the primary and secondary characteristics of culture. The primary characteristics are nationality, race, color, gender, age, and religious affiliation. For example, two people have the same gender, age, nationality, and race, but if one is a devout Roman Catholic and the other is an Orthodox Jew, they may vary significantly in their health-care beliefs and practices. The secondary characteristics include educational status, socioeconomic status, occupation, military experience, political beliefs, urban versus rural residence, enclave identity, marital status, parental status, physical characteristics, sexual orientation, gender issues, reason for migration (sojourner, immigrant, or undocumented status), and amount of time away from the country of origin. Immigration status also influences a person's worldview. For example, people who voluntarily immigrate generally acculturate and more easily assimilate. Sojourners who immigrate with the intention of remaining in their new homeland for only a short time or refugees who think they may return to their home country may not have the need to acculturate or assimilate. Additionally, undocumented individuals (illegal immigrants) may have a different worldview from those who have arrived legally with work visas or as "legal immigrants."	Major influences that shape people's worldview and the extent to which people identify with their cultural group of origin are called the primary and secondary characteristics of culture.	**Yes**. This is copied directly from the source without quotation marks or a citation.
	"The primary characteristics [of culture] are nationality, race, color, gender, age, and religious affiliation" (Purnell & Paulanka, 2005, p. 2).	**No**. It includes quotation marks around exact text from the original source and a citation.
	For example, even with other characteristics being very similar, "a devout Roman Catholic and . . . an Orthodox Jew . . . may vary significantly in their health-care beliefs and practices."	**Yes**. Even though the statement is in quotation marks, the original source is not cited.
	Some secondary characteristics of culture include military service and political beliefs (Purnell & Paulanka, 2005).	**No**. It includes general ideas from the original source and a citation.
	Neither sojourners nor refugees may feel the need to acculturate or assimilate because they both believe that they may return to their home country (Purnell & Paulanka, 2005, p. 3).	**Yes**. Even though there is a citation, the words are still too close to the original. Acceptable: Sojourners and refugees may resist acculturation and assimilation because they see the move as only temporary. (Purnell & Paulanka, 2005, p. 3).

Final Points About Plagiarism

1. One good strategy to avoid plagiarizing is to take notes about your source rather than copying and pasting from the original to your own document. Then use your notes to write the important ideas from the source, as you understand them, without looking at the original source until you have finished.

2. Always remember to make a list of the sources. Follow the style (APA, MLA) that is preferred by your school, and make sure that you include information such as the author, year of publication, title, page or paragraph number in which you found the information, publisher and website for each source. Cut and paste urls from the websites into a document to help you keep track of them. This will also make it easier to create citations in your text and build your reference list.

3. Put quotation marks and mark the page number for *any* text that you have taken directly from a source, even if it is in your notes.

4. Just using good paraphrasing does not eliminate the risk of plagiarism because you need to include the source of ideas in the form of a citation, in addition to the paraphrase.

5. Plagiarism can be confusing for student writers because different readers, such as their instructors, may feel differently about how close is *too close,* in terms of either the source material's language or the original writer's ideas. It is always a good idea to check with your instructor for specific guidelines on plagiarism.

Academic Word List (AWL) Words and Definitions

The meanings of the words are those used in this book. ([U1] = Unit 1)

Academic Word	Definition
academic (adj) [U14] [U19]	relating to schools, especially colleges and universities
access (n) [U18] [U19] [U20]	the opportunity or ability to use something
accessible (adj) [U1] [U19]	possible to reach, approach, enter, or use
achieve (v) [U9]	do or obtain something that you wanted after planning and working to make it happen
acknowledge (v) [U15]	accept the truth or recognize the existence of something
adult (adj) [U14]	typical of, suitable for, or happening to adults
adult (n) [U6] [U7] [U9] [U14] [U15]	a person who has grown to his or her full size and strength; not a child
adulthood (n) [U5] [U7]	the part of someone's life when they are an adult
affect (v) [U2]	have an influence on someone or something
aid (v) [U7]	help or support
alternative (n) [U4] [U13]	something that is different, especially from what is usual; a choice
amendment (n) [U18]	a change or addition to a document
analyst (n) [U4]	someone who studies or examines something in detail, such as finances, computer systems, or the economy
apparent (adj) [U7]	able to be seen or understood
approach (n) [U16]	a way of dealing with something
approach (v) [U15]	meet or communicate directly with someone
appropriate (adj) [U8] [U12]	right for a particular situation
approximately (adv) [U6] [U10] [U14]	almost exactly
area (n) [U3] [U7] [U14] [U17] [U20]	a particular part of a country, city, town, etc.; a particular part of a place or anything that takes space; a subject or activity, or a part of it
aspect (n) [U2] [U6] [U8] [U20]	a particular feature or way of thinking about something
assessment (n) [U12]	a judgment or measure of the quality or importance of something
assume (v) [U8]	accept something as true without question or proof
assumed (adj) [U5]	accepting something as true without question or proof
assure (v) [U9]	promise or tell something to someone confidently or firmly, or cause someone to feel certain by removing doubt
attached (adj) [U2]	feeling close to emotionally
author (n) [U5] [U17]	a writer of a book, article, etc.; a person whose main job is writing books
available (adj) [U15]	ready to use or obtain
aware (adj) [U2] [U3] [U8] [U11] [U17]	knowing that something exists; having knowledge or experience of a particular thing
beneficial (adj) [U20]	tending to help; having a good effect

Academic Word	Definition
benefit (n) [U3] [U5] [U13] [U15] [U17] [U19]	a helpful or good effect; a service provided by an employer
benefit (v) [U15] [U19]	be helped by something or help someone
category (n) [U11] [U12]	a group of people or things of a similar type
challenge (n) [U10] [U16]	something needing great mental or physical effort in order to be done successfully
challenge (v) [U15]	test someone's ability or determination
challenging (adj) [U8] [U13] [U15] [U16]	offering a challenge
cite (v) [U4] [U13] [U16]	mention something as an example or proof of something else
code (n) [U11]	a system for representing information with signs or symbols that are not ordinary language, or the signs or symbols themselves
colleague (n) [U9] [U20]	one member of a group of people who work together
commission (n) [U18]	a group of people or an organization with the authority to gather information, establish regulations, or perform other special duties
commit (v) [U16]	promise to give yourself, your money, your time, etc., to support something
committed (adj) [U14] [U16] [U18]	loyal and willing to give your time and energy to support something
communicate (v) [U20]	give messages or information to others through speech, writing, body movements, or signals
communication (n) [U15] [U19]	the exchange of messages or information; a message, or the process by which a message or information is sent
community (n) [U3] [U14]	all the people who live in a particular area, or a group of people who are considered as a unit because of their shared interests or background
compatible (adj) [U12]	able to exist or work well with something or someone else
complex (adj) [U14]	having many, but connected, parts making it difficult to understand
component (n) [U7]	one of the parts of a system, process, or machine
computer (n) [U11] [U18]	an electronic device that can store, organize, and change large amounts of information quickly
conclude (v) [U13] [U15] [U17]	cause something to end; end; judge or decide something after some consideration
conclusive (adj) [U13]	ending any doubt or uncertainty about a situation
conduct (v) [U3] [U8] [U11]	organize and direct a particular activity
confirmation (n) [U15]	a statement of proof that something is true
consequence (n) [U1] [U4] [U14] [U16] [U17]	a result of an action or situation, especially (in the plural) a bad result
consequently (adv) [U8]	as a result; therefore
consistently (adv) [U18]	in a way that is always similar
consultation (n) [U15]	a meeting with a doctor about an illness or its treatment

Academic Word	Definition
consume (v) [U1] [U13] [U16]	use something such as a product, time, energy, or fuel; eat or drink
consumer (n) [U2] [U13]	a person who buys goods or services for their own use
consumption (n) [U1] [U13]	an amount of something that is used, or the process of using something, especially so that there is less of it
contact (n) [U20]	a person you know who may help you by sharing knowledge or information or introducing you to other people
contemporary (adj) [U9]	existing or happening now
contextualize (v) [U15]	consider something in its context
contrary (adj) [U16]	opposite
contrast (n) [U7] [U8] [U11] [U20]	an easily noticed or understood difference between two or more things
contribute (v) [U10] [U14] [U16]	be one of the reasons why something happens
controversial (adj) [U18]	causing or likely to cause disagreement
controversy (n) [U18]	a disagreement, often a public one, that involves different ideas or opinions about something
conventional (adj) [U11] [U12]	following the usual practices of the past
convert (v) [U4]	change the character, appearance, or operation of something
convince (v) [U2]	cause someone to believe something or do something
cooperation (n) [U15]	the condition of working together with someone
cooperative (adj) [U6]	showing a willingness to act or work together for a shared purpose
core (adj) [U3]	central; basic
corporate (adj) [U3]	relating to a large company
corporation (n) [U6]	a large company
create (v) [U1] [U4] [U6] [U9] [U12] [U15] [U16] [U20]	cause something to exist, or make something new or imaginative
creative (adj) [U5] [U12]	producing or using original and unusual ideas
cultural (adj) [U2] [U3] [U6] [U7] [U8]	relating to the way of life of a country or a group of people
culture (n) [U2] [U3] [U6] [U7] [U8] [U20]	the way of life of a particular people, especially shown in their ordinary behavior and habits, their attitudes toward each other, and their moral and religious beliefs
data (n) [U17]	information collected for use
debate (v) [U18]	seriously discuss or argue the different opinions people have on a particular subject
decade (n) [U4] [U6] [U9] [U16]	a period of ten years

Academic Word	Definition
define (v) [U7] [U12]	describe the meaning of something, especially a word, or to explain something more clearly so that it can be understood
definition (n) [U7] [U11] [U12]	a statement that explains the meaning of a word or phrase
design (v) [U12] [U19]	make or draw plans for something
despite (prep) [U4] [U6] [U11] [U17]	used to say that something happened or is true, although something else makes this seem not probable
discriminate (v) [U14]	treat people differently, in an unfair way
display (v) [U8]	let something become known by what you say or do, or how you look
distinct (adj) [U10]	clearly separate and different
diverse (adj) [U7] [U12]	varied or different
document (n) [U3]	a paper or set of papers with written or printed information
dominant (adj) [U6]	more important, strong, or noticeable
dramatically (adv) [U4] [U9] [U14]	suddenly or noticeably
economic (adj) [U10]	related to trade, industry, and money
economical (adj) [U2]	the careful use and management of money or of time, energy, words, etc.
economy (n) [U10]	the system of trade and industry by which the wealth of a country is made and used
element (n) [U7]	one of the parts of something that makes it work, or a quality that makes someone or something effective
eliminate (v) [U11] [U17]	remove or take away from something
energy (n) [U4]	the power to do work and activity
enhanced (adj) [U13]	improve the quality, amount, or strength of something
enormous (adj) [U12]	extremely large or great
ensure (v) [U11] [U14]	make or be certain about something
environment (n) [U1] [U2] [U3] [U4] [U5] [U6] [U12] [U13]	the air, water, and land in or on which people, animals, and plants live; the conditions that you live or work in and the way that they influence how you feel or how effectively you can work
environmental (adj) [U4]	relating to the environment
environmentalist (n) [U1]	a person who has a specially strong interest in or knowledge of the natural environment, and who wants to preserve it and prevent damage to it
establish (v) [U20]	start something that will last for a long time, or create or set something in a particular way
estimate (n) [U1] [U20]	a judgment or calculation of approximately how large or how great something is
estimate (v) [U20]	to guess the cost, size, value, etc. of something
ethic (n) [U9]	system of accepted beliefs that control behavior, especially such a system based on morals

Academic Word	Definition
ethical (adj) [U3]	good, correct
evaluate (v) [U11] [U15]	judge or calculate the quality, importance, amount, or value of something
exhibit (v) [U5] [U18]	show something, especially a quality, by your behavior
expert (n) [U2] [U4] [U5] [U17]	a person with a high level of knowledge or skill about a particular subject
expose (v) [U18]	create a situation or a condition that makes someone likely to be harmed
exposure (n) [U18]	a situation or condition that makes someone likely to be harmed, especially because the person has not been protected from something dangerous
facilitate (v) [U19]	make something possible or easier
factor (n) [U2] [U9] [U14] [U16]	a fact or situation that influences a result
federal (adj) [U18]	of or connected with the central government of some countries
final (adj) [U2]	last
finally (adv) [U2] [U11] [U12]	at the end, or after some delay
finance (n) [U3]	the management of money, or the money belonging to a person, group, or organization
financial (adj) [U6] [U7] [U17]	relating to money
flexible (adj) [U6] [U8]	able to change or be changed easily according to the situation
focus (v) [U3] [U20]	direct attention toward someone or something
format (n) [U11]	the way in which something is shown or arranged
gender (n) [U6] [U9]	the male or female sex
generate (v) [U14] [U16]	produce
generation (n) [U1] [U9]	all the people within a society or family of about the same age
global (adj) [U8]	relating to the whole world
goal (n) [U3] [U7] [U8] [U11] [U16]	an aim or purpose, something you want to achieve
grade (n) [U20]	the measure of the quality of a student's schoolwork
guideline (n) [U8] [U17]	a piece of information that suggests how something should be done
identification (n) [U13]	the ability to name or recognize someone or something
identify (v) [U12] [U15]	recognize or be able to name someone or something; prove who or what someone or something is
image (n) [U2] [U3] [U19]	an idea, especially a mental picture, of what something or someone is; a picture, such as one seen in a mirror, through a camera, in a photo, on TV, or on a computer
immigrant (n) [U10]	a person who has come into a foreign country in order to live there
immigration (n) [U10]	the process by which people come into a foreign country to live there, or the number of people coming in

Academic Word	Definition
impact (n) [U1] [U2] [U3] [U4] [U14]	the strong effect or influence that something has on a situation or person
impact (v) [U2]	have a strong effect or influence on a situation or person
implement (v) [U3] [U15]	put a plan or system into operation
inappropriate (adj) [U8]	unsuitable, especially for the particular time, place, or situation
inconclusive (adj) [U13]	not leading to a definite result or decision; uncertain
incorporate (v) [U3]	include something within something else
indicate (v) [U5] [U14] [U18] [U20]	show or signal a direction or warning; make something clear
individual (n) [U1] [U5] [U8] [U9] [U16]	a person, especially when considered separately and not as part of a group
initial (adj) [U11]	of or at the beginning; first
insight (n) [U12]	a clear, deep understanding of a complicated problem or situation, or the ability to have such an understanding
insightful (adj) [U5]	having a clear and deep understanding of a complicated problem or situation
instance (n) [U3]	a particular situation, event, or fact
intelligent (adj) [U5]	able to learn and understand things easily
intensive (adj) [U13]	needing or using great energy or effort
interact (v) [U8] [U11] [U20]	communicate with or react to each other
interaction (n) [U6] [U8] [U12] [U19] [U20]	communicating with or reacting to other people
interactive (adj) [U20]	involving a computer user in an exchange of information while a website or program is open
interpret (v) [U8]	describe the meaning of something; examine in order to explain
investigative (adj) [U12]	intended to examine something carefully, especially to discover the truth about it
investor (n) [U3]	a person or group of people that puts its money into a business or other organization in order to make a profit
involve (v) [U11] [U12] [U14] [U15]	include someone or something in an activity
involved (adj) [U8]	interested in or taking part in an activity or event
issue (n) [U7] [U13] [U14] [U15] [U17] [U18] [U20]	a subject or problem that people are thinking and talking about
item (n) [U1] [U2] [U16]	a particular thing considered as one among others of its type
job (n) [U6] [U9] [U11] [U12]	the regular work that a person does to earn money; a piece of work someone does that is of good, bad, or adequate quality
label (n) [U13]	a piece of paper or other material that gives information about the object it is attached to
label (v) [U13]	attach information about an object to that object

Academic Word	Definition
labor (n) [U3]	practical work, especially work that involves physical effort
lecture (n) [U20]	a formal, prepared talk given to a group of people, especially students
legal (adj) [U6]	connected with or allowed by the law
link (n) [U20]	a connection
location (n) [U11]	a place or position
maintain (v) [U2] [U5] [U16] [U20]	make a situation or activity continue in the same way
major (adj) [U6] [U12] [U14] [U18]	more important, bigger, or more serious than others of the same type
majority (n) [U6] [U13]	more than half the total number or amount; the larger part of something
media (n) [U14] [U17] [U18]	newspapers, magazines, television, and radio considered as a group
medical (adj) [U9] [U15] [U17]	of or relating to medicine, or the treatment of disease or injury
method (n) [U11]	a way of doing something
minority (n) [U3] [U9]	a part of a group that is less than half of the whole group; a group of people who share some characteristic by birth that makes their group smaller than some other groups in a society and may cause others to treat them unfairly
modify (v) [U13]	change something in order to improve it
monitor (v) [U18] [U20]	watch and check something carefully over a period of time
negative (adj) [U2] [U4] [U18]	having a bad effect; unfavorable
network (n) [U2] [U17] [U18] [U20]	a group of computers that are connected and can share information; a group of people who share ideas; a company that provides programs to a group of television or radio stations, or both the group and the company
networking (n) [U17] [U19] [U20]	the process of meeting and talking to a lot of people, especially to get information that can help you
neutral (adj) [U8]	not expressing an opinion or taking actions that support either side in a disagreement or war
norm (n) [U8]	an accepted standard or a way of being or doing things
normal (adj) [U14]	ordinary or usual; as would be expected
normally (adv) [U11]	usually or regularly
obvious (adj) [U18]	easily seen, recognized, or understood
obviously (adv) [U19]	certainly, without a doubt
occur (v) [U15]	happen
option (n) [U16]	a choice
oriented (adj) [U12]	directed toward, interested in, or aimed at something
outcome (n) [U8]	the result or effect of an action, situation, or event
parallel (n) [U18]	a similarity between two things

Academic Word	Definition
participant (n) [U8]	a person who becomes involved in an activity
passive (adj) [U5]	not reacting to what happens, or not acting or taking part
percent (adv) [U4] [U14] [U15] [U20]	for or out of every 100
percentage (n) [U17]	an amount of something, often expressed as a number out of 100
perception (n) [U8]	an awareness of things through the physical senses
period (n) [U10]	a particular time during a life or history
persist (v) [U14]	continue to exist past the usual time, or continue to do something in a determined way even when facing difficulties or opposition
phenomenon (n) [U15] [U20]	anything that is or can be experienced or felt, especially something that is noticed because it is unusual or new
physical (adj) [U2] [U11] [U14] [U15]	relating to the body; existing and able to be seen or touched
physically (adv) [U2]	in a way that is related to your body or appearance
policy (n) [U3] [U14] [U20]	a set of ideas or a plan of what to do in particular situations that has been agreed on by a government or group of people
portion (n) [U14]	serving of food
positive (adj) [U3] [U20]	having a good effect; favorable
potential (n) [U11]	an ability that has not yet developed
potential (adj) [U8] [U13] [U17]	possible but not yet achieved
potentially (adv) [U4] [U20]	possibly
previous (adj) [U9]	happening or existing before the one mentioned
principle (n) [U7]	a rule or belief which influences your behavior and is based on what you think is right
process (n) [U2] [U4] [U11] [U12] [U15] [U17]	a series of actions or events performed to make something or achieve a particular result, or a series of changes that happens naturally
process (v) [U15]	deal with something in a known way or according to a particular set of actions
professional (adj) [U11] [U12]	done as a job, or relating to a skilled type of work
professional (n) [U8]	a person who has a job that needs skill, education, or training
promote (v) [U20]	encourage or support something
psychological (adj) [U2]	having an effect on or involving the mind
psychology (n) [U12]	the scientific study of how the mind works and how it influences behavior
purchase (n) [U2] [U17]	something you buy or the act of buying something
purchase (v) [U2]	buy something
pursuit (n) [U3]	the act of following or searching for someone or something

Academic Word	Definition
qualitatively (adv) [U20]	in a way that relates to the quality of an experience or situation
range (n) [U12] [U19]	the level to which something is limited, or the area within which something operates
range (v) [U14]	be limited to a particular length, amount, or area
regulate (v) [U18]	control an activity or process by rules or a system
regulation (n) [U18]	rules or systems used by a person or organization to control an activity or process, or the control of an activity or process
reinforce (v) [U6]	provide proof or support for an idea or opinion
release (v) [U1]	drop, or stop carrying, holding, or containing something
rely (v) [U9]	need or trust someone or something
require (v) [U8] [U11] [U12] [U13]	need something, or make something necessary
research (n) [U4] [U5] [U13] [U15] [U18] [U19]	a detailed study of a subject or an object in order to discover information or achieve a new understanding of it
research (v) [U15]	study a subject in order to discover information
researcher (n) [U12] [U13]	a person who studies something to learn detailed information about it
resource (n) [U1] [U4]	a natural substance such as water and wood which is valuable in supporting life; something that can be used to help you
respond (v) [U11] [U19]	say or do something as a reaction to something that has been said or done
response (n) [U14] [U19]	something said or done as a reaction to something; an answer or reaction
restrict (v) [U3]	limit someone's actions or movement, or to limit the amount, size, etc., of something
restriction (n) [U18]	something that limits someone's actions or movement, or limits the amount, size, etc., of something
reveal (v) [U13] [U17]	make known something surprising or secret
revolutionize (v) [U20]	produce a very great or complete change in something
rigidly (adv) [U11]	in a way that does not permit change
role (n) [U3] [U5] [U6] [U7] [U15]	the duty or use that someone or something usually has or is expected to have
schedule (n) [U8] [U16]	a list of planned activities or things to be done at or during a particular time
schedule (v) [U8]	plan something for a particular time
sector (n) [U13]	an area of activity with its own character that a society, business, etc., is divided into
secure (adj) [U9] [U17]	free from risk and the threat of change for the worse
security (n) [U9] [U17]	freedom from risk and the threat of change for the worse
sequential (adj) [U11]	following a particular order

Academic Word	Definition
series (n) [U16]	several things or events of the same type that come one after the other
shift (n) [U13] [U15]	a change in position or direction
significant (adj) [U2] [U6] [U13]	important, large, or great, especially in leading to a different result or to an important change
significantly (adv) [U8]	in a way that is easy to see or by a large amount
simulate (v) [U11]	create conditions or processes similar to something that exists
site (n) [U12] [U17] [U20]	a website
sole (adj) [U7]	being the only one
source (n) [U13] [U15] [U16] [U19]	the cause, origin, or beginning of something; someone or something from which you obtain information
statistics (n) [U13]	a collection of numerical facts or measurements
status (n) [U20]	a state or condition at a particular time
strategy (n) [U16]	a plan for achieving something or reaching a goal
stress (n) [U14] [U16]	a feeling of worry and fear caused by a difficult situation
stressful (adj) [U12] [U16]	making you feel worried and nervous
structure (n) [U11] [U12]	the arrangement or organization of parts in a system
structure (v) [U11] [U12]	arrange or organize something
style (n) [U7]	a way of doing something that is typical to a person, group, place, or time
subordinate (adj) [U6]	having a lower or less important position
substitute (n) [U4]	the use of someone or something instead of another person or thing
survey (n) [U15] [U20]	a set of questions to find out people's habits or beliefs about something
survive (v) [U9]	continue to live, especially after a dangerous situation
target (v) [U2]	intend to achieve an effect or purpose, or to direct toward a particular person or group
task (n) [U11] [U12] [U16]	a piece of work to be done, especially something difficult or unpleasant
team (n) [U11]	a group of people who work together, either in a sport or in order to achieve something
technical (adj) [U12]	involving or needing special skills or knowledge
technique (n) [U2]	a specific way of doing a skillful activity
technological (adj) [U13]	relating to or involving technology
technology (n) [U19]	the method for using scientific discoveries for practical purposes, or a particular method by which science is used for practical purposes
tension (n) [U16]	anxiety and worry
theory (n) [U12]	something suggested as a reasonable explanation for facts, a condition, or an event
topic (n) [U11] [U15]	a subject that is written about, discussed, or studied
tradition (n) [U8]	a custom or way of behaving that has continued for a long time in a group of people or a society

Academic Word	Definition
traditionally (adv) [U7]	according to tradition
trend (n) [U14]	the direction of changes or developments
unaware (adj) [U2]	not knowing that something exists, or not having knowledge or experience of something
unethical (adj) [U8]	not morally acceptable
unique (adj) [U5]	different from everyone and everything
unstructured (adj) [U11]	not arranged or organized in a systematic way
variation (n) [U5]	a change in quality, amount, or level
vary (v) [U8] [U10]	change or cause to be different
version (n) [U9]	a form of something that differs slightly from other forms of the same thing
via (prep) [U19]	by way of
virtual (adj) [U17] [U19]	happening on or with a computer without going anywhere or talking face-to-face with anyone; almost, but not exactly or in every way
visually (adv) [U20]	in a way that involves seeing or appearance
volume (n) [U19]	the number or amount of something having a lot of units or parts

Glossary of Grammar and Writing Terms

active sentence a sentence that focuses on the doer and the action.

> *People spoke English at the meeting*.

adjective a word that describes or modifies a noun.

> *Large ecological footprints cause problems*.

adjective clause *see* **relative clause**

adverb a word that describes or modifies a verb, another adverb, or an adjective. Adverbs often end in -*ly*.

> *Consumers need to shop **wisely***.

adverb clause a clause that shows how ideas are connected. Adverb clauses begin with subordinators such as *because, since, although,* and *even though*.

> *Some consumers purchase products they do not need **because they are on sale***.

adverb clause of concession a clause that is used to contrast two things or ideas and particularly to indicate that the idea in the main clause is surprising. Adverb clauses of concession are introduced by the subordinators *although, even though, though,* and *while*.

> ***Even though face-to-face communication is preferred**, sometimes business has to be conducted virtually*.

adverb clause of contrast a clause that is used to contrast two things or ideas. Adverb clauses of contrast are introduced by the subordinators *while* and *whereas*.

> *The official language of Brazil is Portuguese, **while in Colombia, it is Spanish***.

adverb clause of purpose a clause that answers the question *why*. Adverb clauses of purpose are most often introduced by the subordinator *so that*, or just *so*.

> *He cut down on fatty food **so (that) he could lose weight***.

adverb of degree an adverb that makes other adverbs or adjectives stronger or weaker.

> *Solar energy is **very** clean*.

adverb of manner an adverb that describes how an action happens.

> *People can get into debt **easily***.

adverb of time an adverb that describes when something happens.

> *Firstborns are generally smarter than siblings who are born **later***.

agent the noun or pronoun performing the action of the sentence.

> *An **interviewer** screens candidates*.

appositive a noun phrase that either defines, restates, or gives important additional information about the noun phrase it follows.

> *John Holland, **a leading researcher in vocational psychology**, developed a theory about career choices*.

article the words *a/an* and *the*. An article introduces or identifies a noun.

> ***A** new family moved in across **the** street from my house*.

auxiliary verb (also called **helping verb**) a verb that is used before a main verb in a sentence. *Do, have, be,* and *will* can act as auxiliary verbs.

*Natural resources **are** becoming scarce.*

*The Earth **does** not have time to renew the resources.*

base form of the verb the form of a verb without any endings (*-s* or *-ed*) or *to*.

come   go   take

citation a statement of the source of information cited, or used, in an essay. It includes who wrote the original material and/or what publication the original material came from.

*"'Car culture,' both in the cities and suburbs, causes the smog that helps make many California cities unhealthful" **("The True Costs of Petroleum: The Community Map,"** 2003).*

citing (in essay writing) stating who wrote the original material and/or what publication the original material came from.

*Producing 20 percent of its energy from wind power, Denmark is the world leader in wind energy production **(Evans, 2007)**.*

clause a group of words that has a subject and a verb. There are two types of clauses: **independent clauses** and **dependent clauses**. A sentence can have more than one clause.

INDEPENDENT CLAUSE   DEPENDENT CLAUSE
Future generations will suffer if pollution is not reduced.

cohesive device a device that a writer uses to connect back to previously stated ideas or information. Cohesive devices include pronouns, demonstratives, repetitions of words and phrases, different word forms, synonyms, and signal words and transition words.

*Visual learners are defined as people who learn through seeing. **For this reason, these** learners need to see the teacher's facial expressions to fully understand the content of a lesson.* (transition expression, demonstrative)

comma splice two independent clauses combined with a comma. To correct a comma splice, you can use a period between the two independent clauses.

Humans cause many environmental problems, it is our responsibility to resolve them. (comma splice)

Humans cause many environmental problems. It is our responsibility to resolve them. (correction)

comparative the form of an adjective or adverb that shows how two things or ideas are different.

*Immigrants in the United States often have **larger** families than Americans.* (adjective)

*Some people talk **more quickly** than others.* (adverb)

complex noun phrase a noun phrase that includes modifiers, such as adjectives, prepositional phrases, and relative clauses.

ADJECTIVE   NOUN   RELATIVE CLAUSE
*Sometimes **professional women who start their own businesses** have trouble getting loans.*

complex sentence a sentence with an independent clause and a dependent clause introduced by a subordinator.

INDEPENDENT CLAUSE   DEPENDENT CLAUSE
Bikeshares are becoming popular because they are a great way to reduce pollution.

compound sentence a sentence with at least two independent clauses that are connected by a coordinating conjunction (*and, but, or, so, yet*). Use a comma before the coordinating conjunction.

There are efforts to clean up the oceans, but the health of our oceans remains critical.

concluding paragraph the last paragraph in an essay in which the writer tries to make an impact. The writer may link back to ideas in previous paragraphs, ask a thought-provoking question, discuss potential consequences, or include a relevant quote.

conditional a sentence that describes a possible situation and the result of that situation. It can be a real or unreal condition/result about the present, past, or future. The possible situation, or the condition, is in the *if* clause.

If companies recycle, employees generally recycle, too. (present real conditional)

If I had read the privacy policy carefully, I would have avoided the problem. (past unreal conditional)

coordinating conjunction a word such as *and, but, so, or,* and *yet* that connects single words, phrases, or clauses.

*Some gases trap heat in the air, **so** the Earth gets warmer.*

count noun refers to a person, place, or thing you can count. Count nouns have a plural form and take plural verbs.

*Large **families** are enjoyable.*

definite article the word *the*. Use *the* with a noun when both the reader and the writer share common knowledge or information about the noun, when the noun is unique, or when the noun was introduced earlier.

*In American families, it is common for **the** wife and **the** husband to share household duties.*

***The** president spoke about mobility in U.S. society.*

*Each person in a family has a moral responsibility to aid other members of **the** family.*

demonstrative the words *this, that, these, those*. Demonstratives are used to show physical distance from the speaker, to show distance in time, or to connect ideas that are close to each other in a text.

*Chapter 2 is about immigration. In **this** chapter, the author describes immigration in the mid-1800s.*

*Immigrants came from all over Europe. Most of **these** immigrants became farmers.*

dependent clause a clause that cannot stand alone. A dependent clause is not a complete sentence, but it still has a subject and verb. Some kinds of dependent clauses are adverb clauses, relative clauses, and time clauses.

***Although people try to save energy**, global use of it increases every year.*

determiner a word that comes before a noun to limit its meaning in some way. Some common determiners are *some, a little, a lot, a few, this, that, these, those, his, a/an, the, much,* and *many*.

***This** unit is about immigration. Let's look at **the** first page.*

*A young Latina woman is **the** new student in **my** class.*

***Few** women are CEOs.*

direct object the person or thing that receives the action of the verb.

*An interviewer screened the **candidates**.*

direct speech (also called **quoted speech**) repetition of a person's exact words. A direct speech statement consists of a reporting clause and the exact words of a person inside quotation marks.

The manager said, "Workers need to use creativity."

-ed phrase a phrase that begins with a past participle that acts as an adjective and modifies a noun.

*Women **elected to Congress** are in the minority.*

element a part of a sentence that works as a grammatical unit, such as a subject, a verb, an object, an adjective, an adverb, or a prepositional phrase.

SUBJECT   VERB PREPOSITIONAL PHRASE

The topic of greenhouse gases is often in the news.

formal a style of writing or speech used when it is not appropriate to show familiarity, such as in business interactions, a job interview, speaking to a stranger, or speaking to a person who you respect. Academic writing is a kind of formal writing.

Good evening. I'd like to speak with Ms. Smith. Is she available?

Swanson (2010) has argued that labeling may be a short-term solution to the problem of GM foods.

fragment an incomplete sentence in which the subject or verb is missing. Avoid fragments by making sure all sentences have a subject and a verb.

In the future, will probably be much warmer on Earth. (fragment, missing subject)

frequency adverb an adverb that describes how often an action happens.

*Ozone and other greenhouse gases are **often** debated in the news.*

future a number of verb forms that describe a time that has not yet happened. The future is expressed in English by *will*, *be going to*, modals, and a variety of words and phrases.

*The Internet **will continue to** allow for a greater exchange of ideas.*

*Some colleges **are going to** ban access to social networking sites on campus.*

*The use of social networking sites by recruiters for jobs **could increase** in the next few years.*

*The company **is about to** introduce a new app.*

future real conditional a sentence that describes a possible situation or condition in the future and its likely result. The verb in the *if* clause is in the simple present, and the verb in the main clause is *be going to* or a modal such as *will* or *might*.

If I get a raise, we will be able to buy a new car.

future unreal conditional a sentence that describes an imaginary situation in the future and gives the result as if it were true. The verb in the *if* clause is in the past, and the verb in the main clause includes one of these modals: *would, could, might*.

If we were socially responsible, we would attract more customers.

gerund the *-ing* form of a verb that is used as a noun. It can act as a subject or object.

***Reducing** our ecological footprints is crucial.*

habitual past a verb form that describes repeated past actions, habits, and conditions using *used to* or *would*.

*I **used to** study on the bus to school every day.*

*While I was living in my country, I **would** go for long walks.*

helping verb *see* **auxiliary verb**.

hook a part of an essay that tries to interest readers and motivate them to keep reading the essay. Hooks may be a surprising fact, a thought-provoking question, or a quotation. The hook is usually the first or second sentence in the introductory paragraph.

identifying relative clause a relative clause that modifies a noun and gives necessary information about the noun. Without that information, the sentence would be incomplete. Do not use commas with identifying relative clauses.

*The study examines characteristics **that are common in firstborn children**.*

if clause the condition clause in a conditional. It describes the possible situation, which can be either real or unreal.

If a company does not make a profit, it will go bankrupt.

imperative a type of clause that tells people to do something. It may give instructions, directions to a place, or advice. The verb is in the base form.

Listen to the conversation.

Don't open your books.

indefinite article *a/an* is the indefinite article. Use *a/an* with a singular count noun when the noun is not specifically identified or when it is first mentioned and new to the reader. Use *a* with consonant sounds. Use *an* with vowel sounds.

*There is **a** new student in my class.*

*The class read **an** article about cultural values.*

indefinite pronoun a pronoun used when the noun is unknown or not important. There is an indefinite pronoun for people, for places, and for things. Some examples are *somebody, anyone, nobody, one, somewhere, anywhere, nothing, everything,* etc. Use singular verb forms when the indefinite pronoun is the subject of the sentence.

Nobody in her family had ever attended college before.

*First, **one** needs to acknowledge that a problem exists.*

independent clause (also called **main clause**) a clause that can be used alone as a complete sentence.

*Although people try to save energy, **global demand for energy increases every year**.*

indirect object the person or thing that receives the direct object.

*Many merchants offer **consumers** green products.*

indirect speech (also called **reported speech**) tells what someone says in another person's words. An indirect speech statement consists of a reporting verb (*see* **reporting verb**) such as *say* in the main clause, followed by a *that* clause. The word *that* is optional and is often omitted in speaking.

The expert said (that) junk food was unhealthy.

informal a style of speaking and writing used to communicate with friends, family, or children.

Hey, there. Nice to see you again.

infinitive *to* + the base form of a verb.

*It is difficult **to find** time to exercise every day.*

infinitive of purpose an infinitive that answers the question *why*. Infinitives of purpose can be introduced by *in order to* and *so as to*. If the meaning is clear, it is not necessary to use *in order*.

*Doctors place brochures in their waiting rooms **(in order) to provide** patients with valuable information.*

*Doctors should discuss treatment options with patients **so as to address** any concerns.*

-ing participle phrase a phrase that begins with the *-ing* form of a verb. It can act as an adjective and modify a noun or it can express cause and effect.

*The number of women **starting their own businesses** is increasing.* (adjective modifying a noun)

Using wind energy, we can lower the cost of electricity. (cause)

*Some countries give tax credits for wind energy, **lowering costs for consumers**.* (effect)

it construction a construction such as *it* + *be* + adjective + *that* clause, *it* + *be* + adjective + infinitive, *it* + *appears/seems* + *that* clause, *it* + *appears/seems* + adjective + *that* clause. These constructions are commonly used in academic writing to make the text more impersonal and objective.

***It is true that** people who exercise usually have more energy.*

***It is important to find** an exercise that is enjoyable.*

***It seems that** people who eat healthier are frequently in a good mood.*

main clause *see* **independent clause**.

main verb a verb that functions alone in a clause and can have an auxiliary verb.

*Solar energy **is** very clean.*

*The government is **investing** large sums of money in alternative energy projects.*

modal a verb such as *can, may, should,* and *will.* It goes before the main verb to show such things as ability, permission, possibility, advice, obligation, necessity, or lack of necessity.

*We **might** buy a hybrid car.*

*The gifts **should** not be expensive.*

modal-like expression a verb such as *have to, be going to,* and *be supposed to* that acts like a modal but changes its form of the verb.

*The country **had to** change its policies.*

*She **was supposed to** major in education, but she decided to change her major to economics.*

modifier a word or a phrase that is added to another phrase to change or describe it. Adjectives, prepositional phrases, and adverbs are examples of modifiers.

*Receptions **for weddings** involve **delicious** foods.* (prepositional phrase, adjective)

*They **commonly** involve music.* (adverb)

noncount noun ideas and things that you cannot count. Noncount nouns do not have a plural form and so use a singular verb.

*My cousin borrowed some **money** from me.*

nonidentifying relative clause a relative clause that provides additional information about a noun. The sentence would be complete without the information in the relative clause. Use commas with a nonidentifying relative clause.

*National Institute of Mental Health, **which is a government agency,** conducts research on the effects of violence on children.*

noun a word for a person, place, or thing.

*Some **consumers** buy "green" **products**.*

noun clause a clause that acts as a noun and that can be the subject or object in a sentence. Noun clauses often start with *that*. They can also start with *wh-* words and *if/whether*.

*Experts suggest **that the consumption of fast food has increased**.*

*Readers have to decide **which experts they trust**.*

*Students who use online sources should check **whether the sources are reliable or inaccurate**.*

noun clause with *wh-* words a clause that starts with a *wh-* word (*who, what, where, when, why,* and *how*). These noun clauses function as nouns and can act as subjects, objects, or objects of prepositions. They use statement word order.

*Students have to learn **how they can evaluate sources**.*

*Experts disagree on **what the benefits of Internet use are for students**.*

noun phrase a phrase that includes a noun and modifiers.

DETERMINER ADJECTIVE NOUN PREPOSITIONAL PHRASE

*The extremely **sensitive issue of gender inequality** has been discussed for many decades.*

object a noun or pronoun that receives the action and usually follows the verb.

*Many researchers study **families**. They analyze **them**.*

object relative clause a relative clause in which the relative pronoun is the object of the verb in the relative clause.

*There are several strategies **that parents can use to help their only children**.*

parallel structure a list in which each item follows the same grammatical pattern.

ADJECTIVE ADJECTIVE ADJECTIVE

*Boys are encouraged to be **aggressive, outgoing,** and **strong**.*

paraphrase to state the information in a different way from the original without changing its meaning.

"Denmark leads the world in wind energy, generating 20 percent of its energy from wind power" (Evans, 2007, para. 3).

Paraphrase: ***Denmark is the world leader in wind energy. Twenty percent of its energy comes from wind power. (Evans, 2007)***

passive a sentence that focuses on the action or on the person or thing that receives the action. The object is in the subject position. The verb form in the passive is a form of *be* + past participle.

The results of the survey were presented by the committee at the meeting.

past modal modals such as *had to/did not have to, should have/should not have, could have/could not have,* and *might have*. Speakers use these modals to give their perspective on past events.

*They **had to** find a way to pay for their education.* (past necessity)

*He **could have** found out about the job opening at the career center.* (possible action in the past)

past participle a verb form that can be regular (base form + *-ed*) or irregular. It is used to form perfect forms of the verb and the passive. It can also be an adjective.

*Researchers have **examined** the situation carefully.*

*Auditions are **known** to be effective interview tools.*

*The **increased** cost of housing has affected many students.*

past perfect a verb form that describes the first of two completed events in the past. It can also describe an action or situation that goes back to an earlier time in a narrative or description. In narrative and academic writing, it is used to give background reasons and explanations for later past events. Its form is *had* + past participle.

*By midnight, he **had finished** most of his work, so he decided to go to bed.*

*Nesreen was nervous on her first day of work. She**'d** never **had** a job before.*

*For years, many people **had considered** the American dream to be achievable. Then the economy changed.*

past perfect progressive a verb form that emphasizes an ongoing past action leading up to a point in the past or a past action that had been occurring when another action took place. Its form is *had* + *been* + verb + *-ing*.

*He**'d been talking** about applying to medical school for a long time. Finally, last January, he applied.*

*They**'d been working** for about an hour when the bell rang.*

past unreal conditional a sentence that describes a hypothetical situation – an untrue situation in the past. Past unreal conditionals describe something that was possible but did not happen. The verb in the *if* clause is in the past perfect. The verb in the main clause uses the modal *would have, could have,* or *might have* and the past participle form of the verb.

If the author had discussed education in his article, the text would have been stronger.

phrase a group of words about an idea that is not a complete sentence. It does not have a main verb.

about the environment

in the future

preposition a word such as *to, at, for, with, of, in, on,* or *above* that goes before a noun or pronoun to show location, time, or direction.

*Stores put snack foods **on** low shelves so that children can see and ask **for** them.*

prepositional phrase a phrase with a preposition and an object, which is usually a noun or pronoun. It can be part of a noun phrase or a verb phrase. Some reduced relative clauses are also prepositional phrases.

*The debate **on immigration** has heated up recently.*

*Immigration has increased **over the past 20 years**.*

present perfect a verb form that describes a past event that is still important in the present. This event may be completed, or it may continue into the future. The form is *have/has +* past participle.

*Some researchers **have demonstrated** that genetically modified food may cause damage to humans.*

*The consumption of GM foods **has increased** significantly in the last 10 years.*

present perfect progressive a verb form that describes an action that started in the past and emphasizes that the action continues to the present and may continue into the future. The form is *have/has + been +* verb *+ -ing*.

*Researchers **have been studying** the impact of GM foods on our health.*

present real conditional a sentence that describes a possible situation or condition in the present and its likely result now. The verbs in the *if* clause and the main clause are in the simple present.

If companies donate to charity programs, they set good examples for other companies.

present unreal conditional a sentence that describes an imaginary situation in the present and gives the result. The verb in the *if* clause is in the past, and the verb in the main clause includes one of these modals: *would, could, might.*

If employees became involved in the community, they would feel good about themselves.

quantifier a word that indicates the amount or degree of something. Some examples of quantifiers are *all, almost all, most, several, some, few, both,* and *no.*

Most toys are gender-specific.

relative clause (also called **adjective clause**) modifies or describes a noun and follows the noun that it modifies. It begins with a relative pronoun such as *who, whom, which, that,* or *whose.*

*Children **who have siblings** are often very close to their parents.*

reporting verb a verb that writers use to report ideas or findings from a source. Reporting verbs are followed by *that* clauses or noun phrases. Common reporting verbs include *say, show, explain, mention, report,* and *state.*

*The authors of the study **conclude** that childhood obesity can be very harmful.*

run-on sentence two independent clauses that are not separated by a period, semicolon, or coordinating conjunction. To correct a run-on sentence, use a comma and a coordinating conjunction to connect the two independent clauses.

Gases trap heat in the air the Earth gets warmer. (run-on sentence)

Gases trap heat in the air, so the Earth gets warmer. (correction)

sentence a complete thought or idea that has a subject and a main verb. In writing, it begins with a capital letter and has a punctuation mark (. ? !) at the end.

The Earth is becoming warmer.

signal words words that help the reader know that the writer has finished writing about one step in the process and started writing about another. Signal words include words and phrases such as *first, the first thing to do, second, next, after that,* and *finally.*

simple sentence a sentence with only one clause, which is called an independent clause or a main clause. Like all sentences, it has a subject and a verb.

Small changes can make a difference.

subject the person, place, or thing that performs the action of a verb.

People should buy less.

subject relative clause a clause in which the relative pronoun is the subject of the verb in the relative clause.

Researchers who study families have different views.

subordinator (also called **subordinating conjunction**) a word that shows the relationship between the two ideas. It introduces an adverb clause. Some common subordinators are *before, after, while, because, since, if, although, whether, whereas,* and *as if.*

Some consumers buy products because they want to be like their friends.

superlative the form of an adjective or adverb that compares one thing or idea to others in a group.

Latinos are currently one of the largest ethnic groups in the United States. (adjective)

Americans are among the groups who say things the most directly. (adverb)

supporting detail a detail or example that explains or supports the main idea of the paragraph.

that **clause** a clause that acts as a noun and that can be the subject or object in a sentence.

The expert recommended that people read food labels carefully.

thesis statement a sentence that states the main idea of an essay and gives a preview of what the writer is going to say about the topic. It is often the last sentence in the introductory paragraph.

time clause a clause that shows the order of events and begins with a subordinator such as *after, as, before,* and *while.*

After I finished high school, I had to find a job.

time signal a word or phrase that makes the sequence of events or ideas easier to follow. They are important in narrative writing. Common time signals are *after, over (the course of), by, for; already, always, ever, just, lately, never; every day, once, once again, twice; later, earlier.*

Over the next 10 years, immigration is likely to decrease.

We've always lived in this neighborhood.

Years later, I returned to Boston to go to medical school.

topic sentence a sentence that introduces the main idea of a body paragraph in an essay. It often appears at the beginning of a body paragraph.

transition word or phrase a word or phrase that connects two independent clauses to make the relationship between two ideas very clear. Transition words and phrases signal a number of different relationships, such as cause and effect, concession, contrast, and steps of a solution. Use a comma after a transition word or phrase.

Environmental values might affect some purchases; **consequently,** *merchants offer green products.*

U.S. executives prefer time limits for meetings. **In contrast,** *Greeks see them as less necessary.*

First, *it is important for people to find an activity that is enjoyable.* **Next,** *they need to commit to doing it.*

verb a word that describes an action or a state.

People **use** *a lot of resources in developed countries. Many of them* **know** *that they should reduce their ecological footprints.*

verb phrase a phrase that includes a main verb, any modals or auxiliary verbs, and elements such as adverbs, direct objects, and prepositional phrases.

               VERB   PREPOSITIONAL PHRASE

Solar energy **will grow in importance**.

Index

Art Credits

Illustration

Bill Dickson: 39, 68; **Shelton Leong:** 27, 253, 262; **Monika Roe:** 34, 101, 286; **Rob Schuster:** 3, 80, 274, 277

Photography

9 ©James Brey/Vetta/Getty Images; 10 ©AFP/Stringer/Getty Images; 18 ©Stewart Cohen/Pam Ostrow/Blend Images/Getty Images; 22 ©Fuse/Getty Images; 38 ©Chris Mueller/Redux; 42 ©Jim West/Alamy; 51 *(left to right)* ©Altrendo images/Stockbyte/Getty Images; ©iStockphoto/Thinkstock; 53 ©PHOTO 24/Photographer's Choice/Getty Images; 56 ©Jim West/Alamy; 57 ©Jens Schlueter/AFP/Getty Images/Newscom; 64 ©Mark Wilson/Getty Images News/Getty Images; 71 ©blue jean images/Getty Images; 72 ©William West/AFP/Getty Images; 74 ©Buyenlarge/Archive Photos/Getty Images; 75 ©Andrew Kolb/Masterfile; 83 ©Sandia/Getty Images; 97 *(left to right)* ©Ariel Skelley/Blend Images; ©Stockbyte/Getty Images; 106 *(top to bottom)* ©Ariel Skelley/Blend Images/Getty Images; ©The Studio Dog/Photodisc/Getty Images; 111 ©Jeremy Woodhouse/Blend Images/Getty Images; 114 ©Christopher Futcher/iStockphoto; 118 ©Ron Chapple Stock/Alamy; 122 ©PhotoAlto/Superstock; 128 ©Saed Hindash/Star Ledger/Corbis; 132 ©Hemant Mehta/Age Fotostock; 136 ©Tetra Images/Tetra Images/Corbis; 138 ©AFP/Stringer/Getty Images; 140 ©Howard Sochurek/Time & Life Pictures/Getty Images; 141 ©Oliver Gerhard/Age Fotostock; 146 ©Lynne Sladky/AP/Wide World Photos; 149 ©ICP/incamerastock/Alamy; 152 ©Lawrence Migdale/Photo Researchers/Getty Images; 158 ©Image Source/Superstock; 165 ©Ariel Skelley/Blend Images; 167 ©Fuse/Punchstock; 172 *(left to right)* ©Jamie Grill/Iconica/Getty Images; ©Adam Gault/Alamy; ©Arthur Baensch/Fancy/Age Fotostock; 180 (left to right) ©ZUMA Press/Newscom; ©Mike Coppola/Getty Images Entertainment/Getty Images; ©Alberto Morante/Newscom; 186 *(left to right)* ©Dan Bannister/Blend Images; ©Jetta Productions/Iconica/Getty Images; 189 ©Gerhard Zwerger-Schoner/imagebroker/Alamy; 194 ©FancyVeerSet21/Alamy; 197 ©Richard Levine/Alamy; 207 ©Donna Day/Stone/Getty Images; 219 ©Hill Street Studios/Blend Images/Getty Images; 223 ©A. Chederros/Getty Images; 234 ©Masterfile; 239 ©Masterfile; 242 ©Martin Novak/Age Fotostock; 243 ©iStockphoto/Thinkstock; 248 ©Don Bishop/Brand X Pictures/Getty Images; 256 ©PM Images/Iconica/Getty Images; 266 ©iStockphoto/Thinkstock; 267 ©Anne Ackermann/Digital Vision/Getty Images; 278 ©Asia Images Group/Getty Images; 291 *(top to bottom)* ©B.A.E. Inc./Alamy; ©Paul Harizan/StockImage/Getty Images; 293 ©iStockphoto/Thinkstock